Original publication: First published in April 2024, First Edition.
(Republished by Amazon Books, 2024)

© 2024 by Karen Felecia Nance

Second Printing

Printed in the United States of America

All rights reserved. International copyright secured. No part of this book may be reproduced, stored in a retrieval system, or transmitted in any form or by any means, whether electronic, mechanical, photocopying, recording, or otherwise, without prior written permission of the publisher, except for inclusion of brief quotations in an acknowledged review.

Ethel Ray Nance: Living in the White, Gray, and Black
by Karen Felecia Nance

ISBN:

Acknowledgement

This biography, as told by Karen Felecia Nance, granddaughter of Ethel Ray Nance, provides a window into the early life of an amazing woman. Ethel Ray Nance was an African American woman who grew up in Duluth, Minnesota, between 1889 and 1923. She and her biracial family endured the challenge in northern Minnesota of creating a community and fostering a place where their family could be free.

DEDICATION

This book is dedicated to my great-grandfather William Henry Ray, to my grandmother Ethel Ray Nance, and to my uncle Glenn Ray Nance.

These three extraordinary souls have left an indelible mark on history and in my heart. Their lives, stories, and unwavering commitment to justice have shaped the narrative of our shared humanity.

To William Henry Ray, who died ten years before I was born, you are a beacon of strength and resilience. Your unwavering dedication to Civil Rights for Black people laid the foundation for future generations to stand tall and demand equality. Your legacy of courage continues to inspire us to challenge the status quo and fight for a more just society.

To Ethel Ray Nance, the remarkable woman for whom this book is written, your spirit burned with the fire of justice. Your unwavering pursuit of Civil Rights and your undeniable strength of character serve as a testament to the power of persistence and the transformative potential of everyone. Your remarkable commitment to the cause of equality has paved the way for progress and lit the path for those to follow.

To Glenn Ray Nance, a custodian of history and a guardian of truth, your invaluable contribution of material for this book has allowed the story of Ethel Ray—your mother, my grandmother—to be told with authenticity and depth. Through your insights and memories, you have breathed life into her journey and ensured her legacy endured.

In Ethel Ray Nance: Living in the White, Gray, and Black, I honor the struggles, triumphs, and sacrifices of each of you.

Through these pages, I celebrate the resilience of the human spirit and the transformative power of love, justice, and compassion.

May this book serve as a testament to your extraordinary lives and inspire generations to come to embrace the fight for equality, challenge prejudice, and live with unwavering dedication to justice. With deepest admiration and gratitude, Your legacy,

Karen Felecia Nance

ACKNOWLEDGMENT

I would like to express my heartfelt gratitude to the following individuals who have played a crucial role in the creation of this book:

Daniel Oyinloye, Henry Banks, Heidi Bakk-Hansen, Rekhet and Anura Si-Asar, and Lenny Prater, for their understanding of the significant contributions made by Ethel Ray Nance, and for continually supporting me in my pursuit of telling my grandmother's story.

Michael Fedo for his groundbreaking work, The Lynchings in Duluth (1976), which shed light on the atrocities committed against three innocent Black men: Elias Clayton, Elmer Jackson, and Isaac McGhie.

To all those mentioned above, as well as the countless others who have assisted along the way, your contributions have been pivotal in shaping this book into what it is today. I am deeply grateful for your expertise, dedication, and unwavering support. Thank you for being an integral part of this journey **and for helping bring this book to fruition.**

LITERARY CONSIDERATION

This publication is a historical narrative based on actual events and actual people that took place in the United States in the late 1800s and early 1900s. This literary work tells a story reflective of the time regarding relationships between the Black and white communities. Within this sphere, the derogatory N-word was used. In this edition of the book, the N-word is used with its full spelling. This may cause visceral responses in readers.

Additionally, there is a photo that spans pages (insert page numbers) of the actual lynching that occurred in Duluth, Minnesota. This image may cause visceral responses in readers. Please skip this page if this is a concern.

Contents

Acknowledgement _____ 4

DEDICATION _____ 5

ACKNOWLEDGMENT _____ 7

LITERARY CONSIDERATION _____ 8

Preface _____ 11

Introduction _____ 17

Chapter 1: AN Immigration/Migration Story in the North Star State _____ 19

Chapter 2: The Formative Years and Young Adulthood ___ 35

Chapter 3: LYNCHING IS AS AMERICAN AS APPLE PIE _____ 52

    THE ACCUSATION: 67

    THE RIOT: 69

    THE LYNCHING: 71

    NEWS COVERAGE: 73

    A WITNESS 77

    THE BLACK GRAPEVINE 79

Chapter 4: Severance _____ 83

    MARITAL CLOAKS 87

    THE NEOPHYTE 95

    MARCH 1921 96

    THE KKK IN MINNESOTA 98

    LEAVING FOR A NEW OPPORTUNITY 98

CHAPTER 5: A PRIVILEGE FOR A LIFE _____ 104

CHAPTER 6: UNYIELDING TRUTH: A LEGACY OF
IDENTITY AND RESOLVE _____ 109

EPILOGUE: A LIFE DEDICATED TO JUSTICE ___ 113

Appendix _____ 115

Timeline _____ 116

Black Population In Minnesota _____ 125

List of Images _____ 128

References And Resources _____ 130

PREFACE

When my grandmother, Ethel Ray Nance, was in her nineties, she gave me many letters and articles documenting her life, and I promised I would write her biography. This is not the book I intended to write. I envisioned telling the complete Ethel Ray Nance story within a single volume; however, I have come to realize several books could be written about her multidimensional life and a documentary made. I decided to focus, in this book, on her childhood and young adult days. I also realized to authentically tell the story of her early life, I needed to travel to Duluth, Minnesota—her birthplace. I made my first trip from my home in the San Francisco Bay Area to Duluth in 2021. While researching her story, I contacted some wonderful people who shared amazing stories.

One story Duluthians shared was shrouded in tragedy, echoing the pain like a haunting presence in the city's past. When my grandmother was just twenty-one, a fateful event unfolded that changed everything. It involved the lynching of three Black men in Duluth. Her family lived just a few blocks away from the location of the lynching. I spoke with Michael Fedo, author of the 1979 book The Lynchings in Duluth, previously titled They Was Just Niggers, and the documentarian Daniel Oyinloye, a longtime Duluth resident, who also produced a short documentary about the lynchings. I felt inspired to add to the historical record of this unfortunate event. The lynchings no doubt reflected life as they knew it back in 1920 Duluth.

My day-to-day life took my focus off the book until my father, Thatcher Popel Nance, Ethel's son, passed away suddenly in 2013. After the memorial service, I found comfort spending time with his brother, my uncle Glenn Ray Nance. He has always been warm, welcoming, and loving. As we talked, I shared my desire to focus on writing my grandmother's life story. Uncle Glenn was supportive and graciously provided me with many additional books and papers he had in his possession that once belonged to Ethel and her father, William Henry Ray. In many ways, it felt like Ethel's love for me was manifesting itself through my uncle. Combing through these hundreds of documents brough moments of healing from the loss of both my grandmother and my father. This book, I hope, is the first of many to honor her legacy.

Ethel Ray married LeRoy Alexis Herbert Williams in Anoka, Minnesota, in 1929. My father, Thatcher Popel Williams, their first child, was born in Washington, D.C. in 1933, followed by their second child, Glenn Ray Williams, in 1934 while the family lived in Minneapolis. After their divorce in 1943, Ethel and the children lost contact with LeRoy. A year later, in 1944, Ethel remarried Clarence Aristotle Nance in Seattle. Clarence served in the United States Navy during World War aboard the USS Mason and later as an electronics instructor during the Koren War. Because Thatcher and Glenn no longer had contact with their biological father, they changed their last names from Williams to Nance following the marriage.

In May 1945, Dr. W.E.B. DuBois, who had formed a close working relationship with Ethel in 1922, invited her to assist him in San Francisco as he served as a consultant to the American delegation at the founding of the United Nations. Leaders from fifty nations gathered there to draft the United Nations Charter, and Ethel agreed to assist Dr. DuBois. The family moved to the Bayview–Hunter's Point area of San Francisco. After the conference concluded, Dr. DuBois, as director of special research for the NAACP's National Office New York, hired Ethel as his research assistant for the remainder of the summer. Later, Ethel returned to San Francisco, accepting a full-time position as special administrator of the NAACP West Coast branches in Hawaii and Alaska.

I was born in San Francisco in 1958. After my parents divorced, I grew up with my father, who did not emphasize a Black identity in our home, and I spend little time with my grandmother or uncle. It wasn't until my high school years, living apart from my father, that I began to develop this consciousness. At fourteen, I moved to Berkeley, California, with my mother, Fannie Mae Westbrooks. She was active in the Black Power movement, the Poor People's Campaign, and many Black community events in nearby Oakland, California. These experiences were crucial in shaping my identity and awakening my consciousness as a Black woman.

Fortunately, my mother encouraged me to spend time with my paternal grandmother, Ethel, who lived nearby in San Francisco. Spending time with her opened my eyes to her remarkable dedication to justice. Ethel was deeply involved in the California Bay Area NAACP-GI Assistance Committee, where she helped raise more than $5000 in 1951 to support Thurgood Marshall, then serving as special counsel for the NAACP. Marshall was investigating allegations of widespread discriminatory court-martials of African American servicemen in Tokyo, Japan. His relentless fight for equality led to his landmark victory in Brown v. Board of Education in 1954, which ended racial segregation in public schools, and later, in 1967, he made history as the first African American Supreme Court Justice. Learning of Ethel's commitment to such important causes instilled in me a deep respect for civil rights work.

Ethel's dedication extended beyond the NAACP. She co-founded the San Francisco African American Historical &

Cultural Society and served on various boards, including the African American Historical Society and the Sickle Cell Anemia Disease Research Foundation. She involved me in her work, and through her connections, I was able to attend the 1975 Black Filmmakers Hall of Fame event-the second Oscar Micheaux Awards Ceremony in Oakland-which celebrated Black filmmakers and honored the contributions of African American artists in front of and behind the camera. It was a glamorous event, with stars like James Earl Jones, Brock Peters, and Ester Rolle presenting awards, and it left a lasting impression on me.

In 1977, my grandmother arranged for me to attend a speech by Alex Haley, author of Roots, during his visit to San Francisco. Meeting him and having him autograph my book that summer after my freshman year of college felt like a profound moment of connections to our heritage. Later that year, participated in Operation Crossroads Africa (OCA), a non-profit, non-governmental organization working to build links between North America and Africa. I was assigned a group in The Gambia-the same country where Haley had traced his ancestral roots. Eager to deepen this connection, I convinced our group leader to travel to Haley's ancestral village of Juffureh, where we met the eldest living Haley ancestor. My journey continued through Senegal, Mail, Burkina Faso, Côte d'Ivoire, and Ghana, expanding my understanding of African heritage.

Returning home, I eagerly shared my experiences with my grandmother, who listened intently, focusing entirely on my stories. She never mentioned that W.E.B. DuBois had invited her to move to Ghana with him and his wife in 1961; her sole focus was always on me and my growth. My grandmother, who was also close friends with Howard Thurman, the renowned author, philosopher, and Civil Rights leader, arranged for me to meet him. Thurman shared insights from his autobiography, With Head and Heart. In addition, Ethel "hired" me to do secretarial work at the

San Francisco African American Historical & Cultural Society, unknowingly paying my salary out of her own pocket. Her support extended even to my school projects; when I once mentioned writing a paper about Frederick Douglass, she handed me a 1963 Ebony magazine featuring Douglass on the cover, saying, "This may be of some assistance to you."

Through her work with the NAACP, my grandmother's fight against the systemic racism embedded in America's institutions of education, public transportation, and public accommodations inspired my eventual path into law. Reflecting on my journey from a young woman to a seasoned attorney with a podcast and published books, I see that my grandmother was quietly preparing me to become a servant to my community and a conscious Black woman, following in her footsteps.

Ethel lived independently in her San Francisco apartment until her early nineties when her mobility began to decline. My father and uncle moved her to an assisted living center forty miles away, but this was far from an end-of-life transition. She continued her work, conducting interviews and sharing over ninety years of memories and accomplishments. During my visits, she would often express a desire to return to independent living, even suggesting once, "Why don't you look into the two of us relocating to the YMCA?" My grandmother was reflecting on the Jim Crow Era (late 1800s to 1960s), a time when segregation laws restricted Black people's access to hotels and public accommodations, making the YMCA a safe haven for Black travelers. I felt tremendous guilt about not being able to grant her wish, and her words lingered as I wrestled with finding a solution.

One day, she entrusted me with a packet of papers, asking me to "hold onto them." I didn't feel any urgency to open it, convinced that she would live to be one hundred. But life had other plans, and she passed away in 1992 at the age of ninety-three.

After her death, I thought of her daily and eventually opened the packet. Within it were treasures—snapshots of her life, reflections, and connections that inspired this book. What you hold now is only a glimpse of her story, pieced together from her packet, newspaper articles, letters, interviews, photos, and keepsakes my Uncle Glenn shared with me.

Ethel Ray Nance is referenced in hundreds of books, articles, and documentaries, yet no book has solely focused on her life and the extraordinary legacy she left as a civil rights activist. She deserves more than a brief mention or a single line in a publication. This book is a tribute to her early years in Duluth, a period when her fighting spirit emerged and her consciousness was shaped under her father's guidance as he taught her to navigate the white, gray, and black of America.

Introduction

"The only Black people in Minnesota are Prince and Kirby Puckett."

—Chris Rock

There is a standing disbelief that Black people would settle in the Midwest, and I don't think this assumption is ridiculous. I can't deny there was a time when Black Minnesotans lay wearily in silence, fearing drowning in a sea of whiteness. Being in the North didn't mean the instinct to survive dwindled. In the early 1900s, in the remote northern city of Duluth, Minnesota, it was hard for Black Minnesotans to keep their heads above water. My grandmother Ethel Ray and her family found themselves victims of violence in both active and passive forms, and they lived through an incredibly frightening mob lynching. The hatred felt by the white residents of Duluth crashed like waves and sparked a race riot, and their rope found three Black necks to break the silence. Black and biracial families shook in rhythm to the sound of swinging ropes, which stretched like twine holding an overbearing weight until they couldn't handle the snap. This separation presented itself in the families capable of dancing between the racial divide. The unions of whites and Blacks created children who squirmed in the awkward gray area and struggled to communicate that none of them felt completely satisfied or safe, so they settled into whatever felt the sanest. For my grandmother Ethel Ray, her parents, and her siblings, that meant a host of things—which manifested in their aspiring for the white, existing in the gray, and living in the black.

Ethel Ray Nance was born in Duluth in 1899 and died in Alameda, California, in 1992. She was the daughter of a Black man from North Carolina and a white Swedish immigrant. Ethel had her grandchildren call her Mormor, the Swedish word for "mother of mother" or grandmother. She learned enough of the Swedish language to communicate with her mother but was not fluent enough to pass it onto her two children. Although she never expressed it, I believed this was Ethel's way of honoring and sharing Great-grandmother Inga with us.

Ethel Ray Nance was a woman of many worlds. She was born in a gray area that could be all-consuming, but Ethel didn't see it as that herself. Even living in between the realities of what came with whiteness and Blackness in American society, Ethel went with what felt right. For her, that was to be Ethel—a strong woman who cared and stood up for others she noticed were suffering. That choice to be completely herself, without fear influencing every action, ultimately led to her embrace of being a Black woman. In this biography, I tell the story of Ethel's rites of passage from birth to the age of 23, when she left Duluth for other opportunities. I also share the backstory of her family and several events that shaped all of them. A look into Ethel's family is required to understand how fear and hesitation can change the course of how one sees one's identity. It only makes sense to start with her parents, who nurtured their children's conflicted spirits.

Chapter 1: An Immigration/Migration Story in the North Star State

In 1888, William Henry Ray scoured the Twin Cities for work. At the time, Minneapolis, Minnesota, was experiencing rapid growth and industrialization. The city's economy was heavily dependent on the lumber, flour, and rail industries. With the growth of these industries came a demand for labor, particularly unskilled workers who could perform manual labor at a low wage.

African American men were seen as a source of cheap labor, and many were recruited from the southern United States to work in northern states. This was part of the legacy of slavery, a large population of African Americans fleeing the South to avoid treacherous conditions and threats to their lives.

As part of the Great Migration, social changes shaped employment opportunities for African Americans. William Henry found a job as a porter at Hotel Ardmore, one of the best hotels in the Minneapolis area. From outside, everything was perfect for him. He was part of a fast-developing African American community in the Twin Cities and was being paid well until he found himself in a situation where he had to flee the dangers of racist men after falling deeply in love with Inga Nordquist, a Swedish immigrant.

William Henry knew of the horrors of the deep South. During his early life in North Carolina, he had witnessed lynchings of Black men for reasons no other than being Black, showing some dignity, or even looking at a white man or woman. Having lost their father and mother, William Henry's older sisters, Peggy and Rachel, believed it would be safer for their ten-year-old brother to move out of North Carolina up North to a place like Ohio, which was known for having some safe spaces for Black migrants. The sisters felt if they did not do something, William Henry would most likely end up being lynched. He could already read and write, thanks to northern whites who had come down to North Carolina and started several schools to teach the newly freed. His sisters could feel the noose slipping around his neck just from the fact he was more articulate and smarter than most of the white men around them. William Henry begrudgingly agreed to leave his family, accompanying some of the people who previously had ensured safe passage on the former Underground Railroad which was a network of routes, safehouses, and resources that helped enslaved African Americans escape to freedom. This trek took William Henry several years. First, he lived in Ohio and later attended South Hill School in Burlington, Iowa. Either in Ohio or Iowa, William Henry was adopted by a German family. In 1888, he arrived in Minneapolis, Minnesota, at the age of 20.

...

Young William Henry Ray, circa 1880s

When Inga Nordquist was eighteen, she left Sweden and came to the United States to join her brother, Louis. Employers wanted cheap help from Europe, and many immigrant girls got jobs in big hotels as maids. Louis set Inga up with a job at Hotel Ardmore as a live-in laundress, a professional who is employed to clean and maintain clothes, linens, and other fabrics. Here, she met my great-grandfather. William Henry was the first man of color Inga had ever laid eyes on, and according to her, he bewitched her with his incredibly good looks. She slowly became aware of the social attitudes towards a couple like theirs. Her Swedish relatives didn't approve of their relationship, and Inga noticed the grimaces when they were together in public. She just wasn't aware of what that disdain could possibly amount to for her partner and herself.

William Henry and Inga Ray, 1889

With the feeling of trouble tightening around his throat, William Henry married Inga in May 1890—but he knew he would still have to run. The idea of a Black man with a white woman, even in Minneapolis, had its repercussions. From the hostility he received from his coworkers and other community folk, William Henry felt that it was a matter of time before a northern noose would be tied around his neck. So, he ran again as he had as a boy from North Carolina, but this time, he ran even farther north to Duluth, Minnesota, with his wife in one hand and a rifle in the other.

Inga Nordquist and William Henry Ray were socially illegal lovers. Even Inga's Swedish relatives felt uneasy about their relationship, and their union was beyond taboo in an American society rampant with racism, yet still they chose each other. It is easy to believe they ended up together due to destiny: A white girl in her teens crosses the waters from the Land of the Midnight Sun, and destiny directs that she marries a young Black man from the segregated South.

William Henry and Inga's first child, William "Will" Nordquist Ray, was born in Duluth in June 1890. Soon afterward, the new family moved another thirty miles up the shore of Lake Superior to Two Harbors, a small town with a population of around a thousand people. The town economy centered around shipping and mining, with many families depending on these industries for their livelihoods. Many children from working-class families worked in the mines or on the docks to help support their families. Here, William Henry and Inga obtained jobs in a boardinghouse.

As the boardinghouse keeper in Two Harbors, William Henry was responsible for managing and maintaining the house, which was a type of lodging that provided temporary accommodation for travelers and workers. Some of the duties he shared with Inga were cleaning and maintenance, which included tasks such as sweeping, mopping, dusting, laundering linens and towels, and preparing and serving meals. William Henry was also responsible for collecting rent from guests, managing expenses, and keeping track of financial records. He was the point of contact for guests and was responsible for ensuring their needs were met and any issues or complaints addressed. Who would've thought someone would put a Negro in charge of such administrative responsibilities?

The family lived in Two Harbors from 1890 to 1898. Their daughter Ora Inga Ray was born in 1893, and their son Oscar Edwin Ray in 1895. Inga was always exhausted from the duties of the boardinghouse and the care of three children, who were five years old and under. When William Henry learned that Inga was pregnant with their fourth child, Ethel, he decided it was time to move, plant some roots, and create some real stability for his family and bought a home in Duluth.

William Henry and Inga found ways to build a life and community in Duluth. Their last child, Ethel May Ray, was born here on April 13, 1899. They connected with other African American families in the area and also found support from sympathetic white allies working to promote racial equality and social justice. However, Minnesota was not immune to the racism and segregation prevalent throughout the United States during the late nineteenth century, and African Americans in Duluth faced many of the same challenges, such as finding or buying a home, as those in other parts of the country.

Together, the family managed the best they could around their white counterparts. There was no shortage of cold stares and ruthless bullying for the kids. For Ora, this racism ended up being lethal.

In 1900, seven-year-old Ora became bedridden with pneumonia. Hospitals in Duluth were limited in terms of their resources and capacity. They were not able to provide intensive care or specialized treatment for pneumonia, nor could William Henry's salary afford hospitalization, so Ora's treatment took place in their home. Inga provided supportive care for Ora and did her best to ensure her daughter was comfortable by providing fluids and nourishment and monitoring her symptoms for signs of deterioration.

As soon as Inga saw Ora's condition worsening, she had her husband summon the doctor. William Henry was home from work when the doctor arrived. The doctor was startled to see a Black man with a white wife and four interracial children. Without examining Ora, he quickly wrote a prescription for her medication and instructed the parents on how much to administer before leaving abruptly. Tragically, Ora died a few days later. Though Ethel was only a small child when Ora passed, years later, she still felt the effects of her sister's untimely death years later. Her mother told her that the doctor who prescribed the medication returned a few days after his initial home visit to find Ora in much worse condition. The doctor scolded William Henry, stating that the dosage he had given was too strong for a sick child and should have been diluted. However, the doctor had not mentioned this when he initially prescribed the medication. William Henry believed that the doctor loathed seeing their biracial family and deliberately omitted critical information about the required dosage to hastened Ora's death.

Ethel's father managed to capture significant moments in the family's lives through photographs. When they laid Ora to rest, he encapsulated the grief his wife and children felt in a photograph. He placed it above the fireplace, and every day, it greeted them with the quote, "Lest we forget." This phrase is taken from Rudyard Kipling's 1897 poem "Recessional." This photograph and phrase served as a constant reminder of the pain they experienced saying goodbye to Ora.

*Will, Inga, and Oscar, after the funeral of Ora
(Photo by William Henry, 1900)*

For the remaining Ray children, living up north was certainly different from where William Henry had grown up in North Carolina. The South may have been a dangerous place to be Black, but at least he had been surrounded by a community of other Black folks. Ethel and her brothers, Will and Oscar, spent a great deal of time with each other, as they found it difficult to integrate with others whose families often disapproved of them and did not allow them in their homes, and many times, would not allow them to play or interact with their children.

When William Henry and his family lived in Two Harbors, he met and became friends with John Beargrease, a legendary figure in the history of Minnesota's North Shore. Born in 1858, fifty miles north of Duluth in Beaver Bay, Mr. Beargrease grew up in a family of Ojibwe and was raised in the traditional ways of his people. His father, Chief Moquabimetem, who also went by the name "Beargrease," had been a renowned dog musher hired by the American Fur Company to deliver mail and supplies to remote outposts. Mr. Beargrease also gained a reputation as a skilled and reliable mail carrier. He was also known for his kindness and willingness to help others. He often carried supplies and messages for people along his route, and he would stop and check on people who were sick or in need. Over time, Mr. Beargrease's reputation grew, and he became a beloved figure in the communities along his route. People began to refer to him as the Great Northern Mail Carrier, and he became a symbol of resilience and determination in the face of harsh North Shore winters.

William Henry's family and Mr. Beargrease's family shared a warm relationship. The Ray children were always excited to watch him use a rowboat and a dogsled to deliver the mail. Beargrease would sometimes bring his oldest daughters, Charlotte and MaryAnn, along to assist him. Other times, his mother, Newagagamsbag (or Otoe), would accompany him. Mr. Beargrease and his daughters would often come into their home to eat, but his mother insisted on staying outside no matter how cold. It was clear she was hesitant about interacting with this Black man, his white wife, and their children. William Henry and Inga were always kind and hospitable, and they wondered why Mr. Beargrease's mother would not enter their home. They would ask, "Why don't you bring your mother in some time? I thought you were going to bring her in?" It turns out she just refused. Several factors may have influenced her decision to stay outside during visits. As a member of a different culture, she might have had values or traditions that prioritized privacy or separation from non-native families.

William Henry loved to share stories with his kids about his adventures with John Beargrease and the other Native Americans in Two Harbors. When hunting together, Mr. Beargrease shared stories about his life and experiences with William Henry. He spoke of his love for the land and his respect for the animals he hunted. William Henry developed a deep respect for his friend's way of life and his people's connection to the land. This connection led him to recall the life he had lived in North Carolina and Iowa before coming to Duluth, and he tried to remember if his people also a similar relationship with the land they had before they were enslaved and forced to work it for free.

Ethel and her brothers did not have many friends in Duluth, but they were no strangers to the Native American children. With them, they could be their full selves. They played together and did not see any difference between themselves and the Native American children. They were all just kids being "wild and free."

This kinship was not true anywhere else. At school and out in their immediate neighborhood, the Ray children began to form ideas of what it meant to be of mixed heritage, of what having a Black father and white mother meant in the context of their world. These ideas planted seeds of doubt in their minds about whether these differences made others better than them. After all, their mother was not just white; her people were Nordic, of Northern European descent. Most white people, including Inga, viewed individuals from the Scandinavian countries (Sweden, Norway, Denmark, and Finland) as having superior intelligence, physical strength, and moral character compared to people from other regions of the world. After Inga mentioned this to her proud Black Southern husband, William Henry insisted that, under his watchful eye, "Black superiority" would be the doctrine of their household. Growing up in the South and fleeing to the North, he was fully aware that white men did not live up to this imaginary image they tried so hard to make everyone believe. If there was anything William Henry felt sure he could control, it was his family. This control would occasionally translate into what felt like a stifling strictness waged against Ethel's brothers, Will and Oscar.

Ethel recognized that corporal punishment was deeply rooted in African American culture, shaped by a history of racial control, including slavery, lynching, and mass incarceration. This context fueled many Black parents' reliance on physical punishment, driven by a real fear of violence from white individuals. By the time Ethel was nine, her only memory of Will, who was nine years older, was that he had moved to Oregon when he was 18. She witnessed Oscar endure blows from their father, and while Will likely experienced similar discipline, Ethel did not see those exchanges. Their mother often intervened, fearing for Oscar's safety. Although William Henry felt remorse afterward, he knew that the punishment he dealt out was minuscule compared to the wrath of racist white men outside their home. Despite her complicated feelings, Ethel loved her father and understood the societal pressures he faced. She yearned to change this reality, but as long as people continued to spew hate and discrimination against others, many Black parents felt they had no alternatives to corporal punishment.

William Henry wasn't hard on Ethel in the same way he was on Oscar. She was frequently ill as a child, and this frailty might have suggested the possibility of a shortened life. In her father's scheme of things, he knew he would be devastated if he was to lose another child.

The tradition of Black families putting fear into their children has direct ties to slavery. Black parents lived in fear of any perceived slight toward white people, which could result in the death of their children. Black people have experienced generations of mental and physical trauma that has taught them that inflicting pain on someone is the key to making them "act right." Making someone fear disobeying rules or not being as topnotch as possible is not the best way to get through to someone because it paralyzes them. Violence is a simple way to keep people in line. When multiple generations are taught that violence works, it can be incredibly hard to escape. Unfortunately, William Henry continued that cycle.

At the turn of the twentieth century, racial segregation and discrimination were rampant in many parts of American society, including housing, education, and employment. The concept of racial purity was also ingrained in the minds of many, and mixed-race individuals were often stigmatized and marginalized. These families faced significant social and economic challenges, including discrimination and harassment from white communities but also nuanced ill treatment from those in the Black community.

The Ray family house kept their children hidden from the outside world. It was as if they were in a perpetual state of quarantine. Neighbors across the street, behind them, and to both sides of them were racist and made it clear they despised the family and did not want them to inhale the air high on the hill. All outings were planned, nothing impromptu. The kids either accompanied their parents to an activity, attended school or church, or spent time with friends who their parents had screened.

William Henry was aware of the limits the racist environment posed on his family and other Black families. Even before the death of his baby girl Ora, he knew the treatment they received was the bare minimum of tolerance. He knew if anything happened, the Black people in his town would not be safe, nor would they have any way to protect themselves and their families.

William Henry began his activism and attempted to establish a NAACP chapter in Duluth in the early 1900's, but many Black residents were opposed. They were afraid it would cause conflict that did not exist, even though a Ku Klux Klan chapter was headquartered in downtown Duluth just blocks from the police station. Little did they know there was trouble on the horizon, and William Henry had every reason to be concerned about the northern town of Duluth.

Chapter 2: The Formative Years and Young Adulthood

All three of the remaining Ray children had differing educational experiences. Will, the oldest, was eight years old when his family left Two Harbors, and he struggled to feel grounded in Duluth. When living in Two Harbors, he had not attended school. Will and his siblings spent most of their time playing with the neighboring Native American children. In Duluth, Will's parents enrolled him in a segregated school, Franklin Elementary, where his fair complexion allowed him to pass as white. He was the only person of mixed race pictured in his class photograph. All the other children and teachers were white. Though Will was able to attend Franklin, his enrollment at the school placed immense pressure on him to navigate his identity in a society that enforced strict racial boundaries. Despite not attending school during his early years, Will kept up with his classmates and later attended Duluth's Central High School in 1905. Central High was an integrated school; at the time Will attended, he was then identified as a Black student. He faced challenges and discrimination that limited his academic and personal success opportunities. Exclusion from extracurricular activities and social events, as well as verbal and physical harassment from white peers, created a hostile learning environment. Yet, Will was able to complete and graduate from Central High.

Oscar struggled in school, not only because of racial discrimination but also internally. He had a hard time learning and fell behind in multiple grades. He struggled with his inability to grow as tall or as athletic as his brother, Will. Ethel surpassed him both physically, growing taller than him, and educationally at the age of sixteen. Oscar grew too embarrassed to continue high school and chose to drop out in his freshman year at the age of twenty-one after discovering he would have to repeat ninth grade yet another year. It is believed Oscar suffered from physical and cognitive disabilities that were not diagnosable at the time. His pride took an irrecoverable beatdown.

There was very little for young people in Duluth. There was one historical Black church at the time, St. Mark's African Methodist Episcopal (AME). Ethel went there occasionally, but her father wanted his children to become regular in their religious habits, so he preferred that they go to the integrated St. Paul's Episcopal Church. There, he said, they would learn regularity and discipline.

Ethel had her share of hostile experiences at school. She was the only student of color at Franklin when she entered, as her brothers had already finished elementary school. She was not able to pass as white as Will or Oscar since her skin was of a darker complexion and she had kinky hair. Even at the young age of five, she was exposed to unfair and racist attitudes. Her desk was placed in the corner at the very back of the classroom. These discriminatory experiences were consistent throughout her early years. This included being cast in a play in which she was the only person of color. Although she was one of the younger and smaller students, she was chosen for the role of wicked stepmother.

As Ethel recalled the events of her early life, she concluded that the complexities and difficulties presented as a member of an interracial family in a small Minnesotan town were made easier to bear through her connection with the church. Dr. Albert Ryan, the minister of the integrated St. Paul Episcopal Church, was very tolerant of young people, including Ethel. She found freedom in the church, and the regimentation of church routine did not present any hardship after the strict discipline she was used to at home. Seven or eight girls constituted the core of the young people in Sunday School, and they remained intact throughout their elementary and high school years, providing Ethel with a cohort of peers. They became a mainstay of helpers when necessary. These experiences helped Ethel develop leadership qualities that will be useful later in her life.

Ethel's father approved the discipline of the established Episcopal church, although he did not attend. William Henry often spoke of the lack of continuity in Duluth's one Black Methodist church, St. Mark's AME, where sometimes there was Sunday School and sometimes not because of a lack of teachers. It was understood in the Ray household that Sundays included attendance at Sunday School unless illness prevented it, then Ethel stayed home. She attended St. Mark's when she wished but only after the regular Sunday School at St. Paul Episcopal. During her high school days, Ethel was elected president of the Philathea Class, the young people's group in the Episcopal church.

Ethel and her brothers were the only African Americans at St. Paul Episcopal for a long time. Another boy and his sister eventually joined them for a short period. Dr. Ryan's influence must have generated a friendly environment compared to other white churches.

World War I started in 1914, and the United States voted to enter the war in 1917. Both Will and Oscar enlisted in World War I in 1918. They both ended up in France after the end of the war in 1919. Ethel's desire to leave Duluth grew after seeing her brothers leave not just the state but the country, but Ethel's desire to leave Duluth grew.

Prior to graduation, Ethel watched a close white friend named Adaline quit high school after she acquired a full-time job at a department store. On the other hand, Ethel was advised by her family and friends to stay in school. She couldn't quit school to work even if she wanted to, as there were little to no job opportunities in Duluth for Negroes. On June 13, 1917, just two months after the start of America's involvement in World War I, Ethel graduated from Central High School. She held onto the graduation program from which her name was inauspiciously absent. However, her senior class picture appeared in the yearbook, and her accomplishments were listed alongside it. Her many accomplishments included learning stenography (a note-taking technique) and having near-perfect scores on the civil service examination.

In October 1918, the year after Ethel graduated from high school, disastrous forest fires took the lives of more than five hundred people in northern Minnesota, injured about two thousand people, caused more than thirty million dollars in property damage, and devastated several entire communities as well as a million acres of forestland. Over eleven thousand families became homeless refugees. More than four thousand homes and over six thousand other buildings were destroyed. Workers were needed at the emergency relief headquarters in Duluth. The governor appointed a Minnesota Forest Fire Relief Commission to work in cooperation with the American Red Cross. Colonel Hubert V. Eva, the state director, was in charge.

Calls went out from Moose Lake for volunteers, and Ethel applied. Luckily, she had worked under Colonel Eva during the Liberty Loan Drive. He hired her immediately upon her arrival at headquarters as an investigator to interview refugees and as a stenographer in Moose Lake, forty miles southwest of Duluth. Ethel worked in this capacity from October 1918 to March 1919. Her duties, along with many other volunteers, included checking emergency relief centers and hospitals for lists of survivors and morgues for lists of the dead, with whatever descriptions were available. Information was sparse, such as a "few inches of a braid of blond hair," "a small piece of a gingham dress," and "part of a shoe." Food, clothing, and shelter were priorities. In addition to her work as an investigator and stenographer, Ethel worked with Charles F. Mahnke, the Editor of the Moose Lake Star Gazette.

The same year as the forest fires, an influenza epidemic closed the schools. Since schools were closed, teachers were drafted into service to locate and interview refugees. They reported each morning for their daily assignments. Ethel ended up running into her former third-grade teacher, who had discriminated against her when she was younger. This teacher was now assigned to Ethel, who supervised her and gave her daily appointments. Ethel doubted this woman had any recollection of who she was as she did not appear to recognize her. Nonetheless, the irony was not lost on Ethel.

After the assignment ended, Ethel went back home to Duluth looking for work. A couple of months later, Charles F. Mahnke, who was also the local director of the forest fire relief commission, had a position open in Moose Lake. A worker from Chicago had become ill enroute to Moose Lake, so Ethel volunteered to go back down to serve temporarily. She had previously worked for Mr. Mahnke as his secretary, assisting with his work as the editor of the Moose Lake Star-Gazette weekly newspaper. He was also chairman of the school board, chairman of a building committee for the Methodist church, and a representative of the Federal Loan Bank.

Moose Lake was a community that had been seriously hit by the tragedy and held the highest mortality rate in the state. The forest fires had leveled the town, like the images that had come out of World War I's devastated cities in Europe. Temporary barracks were built for housing and for office quarters. The town was under the military jurisdiction of the Minnesota Home Guard.

After her temporary assignment ended, Mr. Mahnke asked Ethel to return for a permanent assignment in Moose Lake. Ethel's parents reluctantly agreed since the opportunity would provide her with valuable work experience; however, William Henry thought the people of Moose Lake were getting exactly what they deserved for being the most racist stop on the railroad for Black men who worked the route from Duluth to Minneapolis. His stance was by no means an unusual occurrence. Moose Lake was known by many to be a racist town, but Ethel, left with limited options had to work wherever the opportunity arose.

Ethel lived in Moose Lake for about three years, from 1919 to 1922. The state was divided into fire relief districts, and weekly meetings were held at headquarters in Duluth to bring together all directors in charge of area relief. Although social workers had been brought in from all over the country, the flu epidemic kept the working force seriously understaffed, so Ethel was able to visit home only on rare occasions.

The workers were kept busy by the lines of people coming into the office for food, clothing, and lumber to build temporary homes. Below-zero temperatures made it necessary to work in topcoats until wood fires could be started each morning in the offices. Ink wells were frozen, and typewriter keys refused to respond to touch until midday.

While Ethel lived in Moose Lake, she attended the local Methodist church since the Episcopal church held services only once a month. She became active in Sunday School and played the organ. She was eventually elected president of the Epworth League, the Methodist young people's organization. The young people at the church in Moose Lake were active in giving programs for other organizations and in adjoining towns. Ethel also became president of another group called the Loyal Chums.

Despite her extensive experience and skills, like many Black students, Ethel had little chance of earning a scholarship or gaining admission to college without a recommendation from someone influential. Mrs. Elva Jackman, the superintendent of the Moose Lake Episcopalian Sunday Schools, recognized Ethel's potential and acted. She wrote to New York to request permission for Ethel's consideration for admission and reached out to the state Sunday School Association, hoping to secure a scholarship to make college possible for her.

Shortly afterward, the superintendent of Sunday Schools at the Episcopalian church in Duluth learned of Mrs. Jackman's efforts and reached out to Ethel. After interviewing her, he mentioned that arrangements could potentially be made for her to attend either the Episcopal Institute in New York City or a religiously affiliated branch of Boston University. Ethel, thinking practically, asked if the institution would help graduates find jobs. He replied that she would likely be assigned to work with Indigenous communities in northern Minnesota or Black communities in Asheville, North Carolina. His response felt discriminatory; it was clear that, despite countless employment opportunities across the country, her options were limited solely because she was Black. Discouraged, she set the matter aside. Her parents, too, disapproved of the Boston and New York options, as they were reluctant for her to be so far from home.

As life in Moose Lake settled back into a rhythm after the fire's aftermath, Ethel noticed the subtle and overt discrimination around her more sharply. When social gatherings resumed, members of a women's life insurance society, known as the Degree of Honor Club, urged her to join. Though not particularly interested, Ethel considered it as a way to ease her loneliness. The local barber, originally from Kentucky, voiced his disapproval, telling the women that his wife would not join if a "Negro" was allowed membership. Nevertheless, the women who had nominated Ethel insisted on her inclusion.

In the small town, stereotypes about Black people persisted. Some residents assumed that Ethel could sing and fry chicken, simply because "all Negroes do and can." One evening, she was invited to join a group of young people in "cooning" melons—a term they used for sneaking onto farmers' land to take melons. Ethel declined.

Other encounters were equally demeaning. A dentist in a neighboring office who often visited the relief center enjoyed telling "amusing" stories about Black people. He once claimed that Black people's teeth only appeared white because of the contrast with their skin, insisting that their teeth were usually yellow. The dentist, who had once performed in blackface, seemed to revel in these offensive demonstrations.

Despite these challenges, Ethel felt fortunate to work under Mr. Mahnke, who exhibited no prejudice toward her or anyone else. He respected the town's only Jewish family, who ran the clothing store, and valued the many Finnish immigrant farmers, who spoke little English and often turned to him in emergencies. Mr. Mahnke valued Ethel's work, and his appreciation made her time in Moose Lake bearable. Yet outside of work, the loneliness weighed heavily on her, as the isolation from genuine companionship remained constant.

The Pilgrimage (December 1919 to March 1920)

Negro college students came to Duluth during the summer months to work on the docks by the ships. Ethel remembered some arrived on ships named the SS (Steam Ship) Juniata and the SS (Steam Ship) Octorara, part of the Great Lakes shipping fleet, primarily transporting cargo such as iron ore and grain. Duluth served as a significant port for these types of ships, contributing to the region's economic growth during that time. Duluth, with its strategic position at the southwest tip of Lake Superior, was a key port contributing to the region's economic growth. The city itself stretched over a mile high and fourteen miles long, perched on a hillside overlooking the lake. It was a beautiful sight to watch the ships arrive and depart from the port.

Duluth was often compared to its neighboring city, Superior, Wisconsin. Known collectively as the Twin Ports, the two cities were separated by the St. Louis Bay bridge. Despite their proximity, a notable difference existed between them. Superior, with a largely German population, had a more favorable attitude toward Black people than Duluth, which was predominantly Scandinavian. There were few Black residents in either Superior or Duluth, just as there were few in most of the places where the Rays had lived, many young people left the area due to the lack of opportunities and activities.

Social gatherings were scarce. The Rays would occasionally visit a place known as "The Point," a strip of land across the Aerial Bridge on Lake Superior. Many Duluth residents enjoyed crossing the bridge for picnics, but Ethel and her brothers were forbidden from using the word "picnic." Their father, William Henry, who was well-read, explained that while the word "picnic" derived from the 17th-century French word "pique-nique," referring to a social gathering where everyone contributed food or useful items, there was another interpretation tied to racial history. He explained that some people believed the word was racist because it had been associated with the phrase "pick a" followed by a derogatory slur for a Black person. According to this belief, the phrase referred to the horrific act of choosing a Black person for lynching or other violence, during which white people would feast. While William Henry knew the true French origin of the word, he was sensitive to the painful connotations it carried for many in the Black community, and thus, the word was not used in their household.

But aside from the Sunday school gatherings or the occasional get-togethers among a few families, there wasn't much for young people in Duluth. Things were a bit livelier when the teenagers organized their own dances and house parties. In the summertime, students from Howard, Fisk, and other Southern Historically Black Colleges and Universities (HCBU) would visit Duluth during the day and spend their nights in nearby Superior. Matinee dances were held, with mothers chaperoning the events, offering a welcome social outlet for Ethel and her friends.

William Henry was aware that the young Black men who came to Duluth for summer jobs from prestigious colleges across the country held a certain appeal for Ethel. He didn't want her to be swept off her feet by someone she believed could show her the world. William Henry wanted to be the one to open her eyes to the world beyond Duluth, to share the broader experiences and knowledge that he felt were essential for her growth. With that in mind, he decided to take Ethel on an extended trip to the Northern states and down South. The timing was perfect for Ethel, who was working in Moose Lake and had accumulated a significant amount of paid leave. William Henry saw this trip as both an opportunity to educate her about her heritage and a chance to meet her distant relatives in North Carolina.

Her mother did not want Ethel to go. Inga knew it wasn't safe for a Black girl in Duluth but feared what could happen to her daughter in the South. She had heard stories of why her husband fled the South and the terrible discrimination he faced. But William Henry said they were going, and the two of them went.

Ethel's first journey outside of Minnesota in 1919-1920 was a transformative experience that shaped her perspective on race, community, and her own identity. For the first time, she traveled through major American cities, meeting Black leaders, exploring historic sites, and witnessing the daily lives of Black communities across the country. Accompanied by her father, who meticulously planned the trip, Ethel visited cities like Chicago, Detroit, Boston, New York, Philadelphia, Baltimore, Washington, Raleigh, and Atlanta. The purpose of the journey was not only to acquaint Ethel with urban life but also to introduce her to the rich legacy of Black accomplishments in the United States.

The journey began in Chicago, and Ethel was immediately struck by the city's towering skyscrapers and bustling streets. It was unlike anything she had seen before. Walking along State Street, she marveled at the vibrant

Black community, witnessing a thriving neighborhood filled with Black-owned businesses, families, and young people who seemed comfortable and confident in a way that was rare in Duluth. For Ethel, Chicago represented a world of possibilities and promise, especially as she saw places like the Illinois Central YMCA, which provided recreational space for Black residents. The sense of pride and solidarity she felt in Chicago's Black community left an indelible mark on her, contrasting with the more limited environment she was used to in Minnesota.

From Chicago, Ethel and her father traveled through Toledo, Detroit, and Buffalo, each city offering new glimpses of the Black experience. In these industrial cities, Ethel observed the complexities of urban life for Black communities—on one hand, the opportunity to earn a living, and on the other, the challenges of racial discrimination. Yet, she was inspired by the resilience of the people she met and the sense of community they had fostered in these northern cities. Each stop added a new layer to her understanding of what it meant to be Black in America, and the shared struggles and triumphs she saw began to reshape her view of herself and her place within this broader community.

Boston was a particularly powerful stop for Ethel. She was captivated by the city's historical richness, especially as it related to the nation's early Black history. She visited landmarks like the Crispus Attucks memorial and the Boston Commons, sites that honored Black contributions to the American Revolution and symbolized the sacrifices Black people had made for the nation's freedom. These historic sites filled Ethel with a profound sense of pride and reverence for those who had come before her, people who had paved the way for justice even in the face of adversity.

In Boston, Ethel also encountered a thriving Black intellectual community. She met Monroe Trotter, editor of The Guardian, one of the country's most prominent Black newspapers. Through conversations with Trotter and other local activists, Ethel began to understand the power of the press in advocating for social change. She saw how Black newspapers provided a voice for those who had been marginalized, offering a platform to challenge injustice and to celebrate Black excellence. These encounters sparked her own interest in activism, as she realized that writing and journalism could be powerful tools for empowerment and change.

New York City was another significant destination for Ethel. In Harlem, she experienced the heart of the Harlem Renaissance, a burgeoning cultural movement that celebrated Black art, literature, music, and intellectual life. Ethel visited the offices of the Messenger and the Crisis, where she met influential figures like A. Philip Randolph and other prominent leaders who were fighting for racial equality and workers' rights. Witnessing Harlem's vibrant artistic and intellectual life left a profound impact on Ethel, revealing the transformative power of culture and community in the fight for social justice. The sense of unity and creativity that permeated Harlem resonated deeply with her and showed her that Black communities were not only surviving but thriving, challenging stereotypes and asserting their rightful place in American society.

As she traveled south, Ethel encountered both warmth and stark reminders of racial divides. Raleigh, North Carolina, was a particularly meaningful stop. For the first time, she connected with her family's Southern roots, visiting relatives she had only heard about in stories. Her father took her to see a piece of family land he had been working hard to retain, despite the financial strain it placed on their family in Duluth. This land, and the relatives who lived nearby, connected Ethel to a deeper heritage, grounding her in a history she had previously only heard in fragments. The visit to Raleigh also offered her a rare opportunity to engage with her family's history in the South, a connection that instilled in her a sense of pride and responsibility.

While in Raleigh, Ethel took the chance to substitute for a cousin who taught in a rural school. The school, though small and modestly furnished, was filled with young Black students eager to learn. This experience was eye-opening for Ethel, as she witnessed firsthand the dedication of Black educators and the resourcefulness of the community in providing education for its children despite limited resources. The warmth and gratitude she felt from the students and their families were deeply moving, solidifying her appreciation for the resilience and strength of her people. This brief experience as a teacher awakened a sense of duty in Ethel, inspiring her to find ways to give back to her community.

Throughout her travels, Ethel encountered a wide range of attitudes toward Black people. In the northern cities, while discrimination existed, she saw a degree of acceptance and, more importantly, thriving Black communities that had carved out spaces of support, culture, and empowerment. In the South, however, racial discrimination was often more overt. Limited job opportunities, segregated facilities, and condescending attitudes reminded her of the deeply ingrained racial divides that persisted in society. Despite these challenges, Ethel was inspired by the resilience and pride of the Black communities she encountered. Whether it was the thriving cultural scene in Harlem or the dedicated educators and students in rural North Carolina, she saw strength and determination that affirmed her belief in the potential for progress and justice.

Each city revealed new facets of the Black experience in America. Visiting places like Atlanta University, Morehouse College, and Spelman College in Atlanta, Ethel saw the importance of Black educational institutions in the South. These schools served as havens of learning, leadership, and community, and she was inspired by the students and faculty who were dedicated to fostering the next generation of Black leaders. Atlanta, known as the "New York of the South," showed Ethel the power of education as a tool for advancement and empowerment. She saw how these institutions were nurturing Black excellence and laying the groundwork for future progress.

By the time Ethel returned home, her perspective on her own identity and her place within the Black community had been forever changed. She returned to Duluth with a newfound pride in her heritage and a deepened commitment to contribute to the broader struggle for justice and equality. The journey had introduced her to the strength, resilience, and accomplishments of Black Americans across the country. She had seen the beauty of Black culture, the power of community, and the importance of self-determination. This transformative experience solidified her resolve to serve her community and work for positive change.

Ethel's journey was a defining moment, one that would inspire her lifelong dedication to social justice and equality. She returned to Duluth with a sense of purpose and a vision for her role within the larger Black community. The lessons she learned from the people she met, the institutions she visited, and the history she absorbed would guide her as she sought to make a difference in her own community, carrying forward the legacy of Black progress and empowerment. This journey not only broadened her horizons but also ignited a passion within her that would shape her path for years to come.

Chapter 3: Lynching is as American as Apple Pie

Although lynching had been America's practice in maintaining fear and control since the country's founding in 1776, when the enslavement of African people was legal, the owners of African people did not see fit to lose their investments by destroying their "property." Black bodies were valuable commodities after they reached American soil. It wasn't until after the Civil War ended in 1865 and the physical freedom of enslaved Africans that a new level of terror was visited upon the barely freed. A Black body was no longer something to be commodified, so the torture a white man inflicted didn't have to stop at the brink of death. A white man could kill a Negro, and there wasn't any good reason to stop him. After Reconstruction ended in 1877, Union troops were pulled out of the South, which allowed for the full reign of the Ku Klux Klan, and the frequency of the lynchings of Black men increased exponentially.

Ida B. Wells, a pioneering Black woman, dedicated her life to documenting the horrors of lynchings across the country. In her 1909 speech, "Lynching, Our National Crime," she detailed 959 lynchings that occurred between 1899 and 1908. Of those victims, 102 were white, while 857 were Black. This amounted to nearly two Black men being lynched every week during that nine-year period. By the summer of 1919, when Ethel was working in Moose Lake to help white communities recover from devastating fires, racial violence against Black people had intensified to such a degree that it became known as the "Red Summer." In more than three dozen cities across the country, white supremacist terrorism reigned. From 1882 to 1968, records kept by the NAACP reveal that 4,743 lynchings occurred in the United States, with 72 percent of the victims being Black. This violence was fueled by the false myth of race and white supremacy, which perpetrated the belief that Black men posed a threat to the "purity" of white women. In the eyes of many, even the mere act of a Black man looking at a white woman was enough to justify immediate, brutal death.

Minnesota-and in particular, Duluth, a populist northern city-was not exempt from the lynching culture that permeated the rest of the country. While the history of lynching in 1920 in Duluth, Minnesota, it reached its most brutal and visible point that year. Billie Holiday famously sang of Southern trees bearing strange fruit, but Bob Dylan's lyrics in "Desolation Row" revealed that the North, too, had its own gruesome legacy, as postcards from Duluth depicted the lynching of Black men. This was not merely a Southern phenomenon.

On June 15, 1920, Duluth residents dragged, beat, and lynched three young Black men in a horrific public spectacle. Their bodies were not hung from trees in pastoral fields but from a wooden telegraph post against the backdrop of the Shrine Temple and the cityscape of Duluth. These men, barely out of their teenage years, were subjected to mob violence in a state as far north as one could go before crossing into Canada. Photographs were taken at what was chillingly referred to as "the necktie party," a grotesque event that highlighted how quickly the life of a Black man-particularly a Black circus worker-could be ended by the whims of a racist mob.

The Circus is Coming to Town

Each year, Duluth hosted John Robinson's Circus, a well-known Midwest family circus that lasted seventy-five years until 1917, when it was acquired by the American Circus Corporation. By 1920, under new ownership, the circus came to town with its usual array of tents, trapeze artists, lions, tigers, elephants, clowns, and cotton candy. The circus moved almost daily, visiting multiple towns each week, with two performances a day, from spring until late fall. For the workers, especially the Black laborers known as "roustabouts," life was anything, but the excitement seen under the big top.

Figure 3.1

The world of the circus, seen by audiences as a place of wonder and joy, held a darker, more grueling reality for the Black workers who labored behind the scenes. Known as "roustabouts," these men were responsible for the most physically demanding and dirty tasks, such as setting up and tearing down tents, hauling equipment, and managing animals. Numbering between twenty and fifty, they were paid less and subjected to harsher treatment than their white counterparts, living in segregated train cars and often facing discrimination, hostility, and danger in the small towns they visited. For these Black laborers, the circus offered employment, but it came at a high price, with backbreaking labor, low pay, and constant exposure to racial violence.

The circus culture itself reinforced this harsh treatment. Black workers were relegated to the lowest-status roles, such as stable hands, cooks, cleaners, and later, musicians—but even then, they were paid as little as possible. Their labor was considered expendable, and their safety was rarely a priority. A chilling example of this expendability occurred in 1892 when a circus train accident claimed the lives of fourteen horses, while most of the Black roustabouts in the same cart survived. Yet, instead of expressing relief or gratitude for the workers' lives, the media and circus management lamented the loss of the animals. The newspaper coverage of the incident led with the headline "Horses Better Than Negroes," reflecting the manager's greater concern for his valuable horses than for the lives of his Black employees, whom he dismissed as "darkies." This incident starkly illustrated the depths of dehumanization these men faced in the circus world, where Black workers were viewed as tools rather than human beings. The African

Dodger game, a grotesque form of entertainment in early 20th-century circuses and carnivals, was a public display of brutality masked as amusement. For the price of five cents, carnival-goers could buy the opportunity to hurl a baseball at the face of a Black man, who was forced to stick his head through a hole and endure the blows. These Black men, called "Dodgers," had no chance to avoid the balls, despite the name of the game. They were required to keep their heads exposed, knowing that every throw brought them closer to serious injury. For many, this cruel spectacle left permanent marks on their bodies and spirits, as fractured jaws, shattered noses, and damaged eyes were common outcomes of their repeated exposure to this violence. However, for the crowds that gathered to participate, these injuries were simply part of the spectacle, a source of added excitement for those who saw the Dodger's pain as part of the price of admission.

The injuries sustained by these men were severe, yet they received no medical treatment, no compensation, and no care from those who organized or profited from the game. Instead, these Black men were left to endure their suffering in silence, often without the means to recover properly. The scant payment they received for their participation in the game was a fraction of the carnival's profits, and it did not even begin to cover the costs—physical, emotional, or financial—of the injuries they sustained. Many "Dodgers" were permanently disfigured, their lives irrevocably altered for the brief amusement of a crowd that saw them as less than human.

The newspaper articles that covered their injuries often did so with a sense of detachment, if not outright amusement.

Rather than sparking outrage or sympathy, these reports were presented as another form of entertainment for those who might have missed the event. The coverage reinforced the public's view of these men as objects of ridicule rather than individuals deserving of dignity and care. This practice revealed a profound cultural indifference to the bodily harm inflicted on Black men for entertainment, treating their suffering as something to be trivialized or ignored.

The African Dodger game was emblematic of the broader dehumanization that Black men faced in the circus industry. Black roustabouts, who were relegated to the hardest, dirtiest, and most dangerous jobs within the circus, were similarly seen as expendable labor. Paid less than their white counterparts and kept segregated in separate train cars, these men were expected to carry out backbreaking work under grueling conditions, all while facing daily racial hostility. The circus management viewed their Black laborers as little more than tools, essential to the circus's operations but entirely disposable. Their lives were treated with the same disregard as those of the African Dodgers—both groups were exploited, mistreated, and offered no medical care for their injuries.

This dehumanization was starkly illustrated in the circus world's reaction to an 1892 train accident, where fourteen horses were killed alongside injured Black roustabouts. The circus manager publicly lamented the loss of his valuable horses, while the Black men who survived were scarcely acknowledged, let alone cared for. The headline that followed, "Horses Better Than Negroes," captured this horrifying reality: for the circus industry and many within society, the lives of Black men were deemed less valuable than those of animals. The circus industry and its audiences profited from the labor and suffering of Black men, yet these men were denied even the most basic medical treatment or compassion when they were hurt or in need.

This broader culture of dehumanization and disregard reached its apex in the lynching of Elias Clayton, Elmer Jackson, and Isaac McGhie in Duluth on June 15, 1920. These young Black men, who traveled north with the John Robinson Circus, may have hoped that life in the Midwest would offer a respite from the dangers they knew in the South. However, when a young white woman falsely accused Black men from the circus of assault, the pervasive racial hostility that simmered beneath the surface of northern society erupted into a violent lynching. Without evidence or trial, Clayton, Jackson, and McGhie were jailed, then brutally taken by a mob of thousands who stormed the police station, determined to exact their own form of "justice."

The lynching of these men was a grotesque public spectacle, eerily reminiscent of the African Dodger game in its callous disregard for Black lives. The crowd beat, tortured, and hanged them from a telegraph pole in the middle of Duluth, transforming the event into a perverse form of communal entertainment. As with the African Dodger game, injuries were inflicted without care or concern, and the men's suffering was treated as a sideshow for the amusement of the mob. Photographs were taken of the hanging bodies, and these images were later printed as postcards and sold, reinforcing the culture that saw Black pain and death as consumable commodities.

For Black circus workers like Clayton, Jackson, and McGhie, the constant travel from one town to the next offered little protection from the racial hatred that permeated American society. They knew that their lives were precarious, that at any moment, a baseless accusation or violent whim could lead to their deaths. Their work for the circus, though essential, afforded them no safety, no stability, and no defense against the mob's brutal, racist violence. The tragedy in Duluth made it painfully clear that even in the supposedly progressive North, Black men's lives were viewed as expendable.

The events in Duluth exposed the harsh truth that Black people in America were often seen not as human beings but as targets for white anger, tools for white profit, and objects for white entertainment. The lynching, like the African Dodger game and the disregard shown for injured Black roustabouts, underscored a society willing to exploit and harm Black individuals without consequence. The systemic failure to protect, treat, or value these lives was a reflection of the broader, entrenched racism that governed American life.

This legacy continues to challenge us today. The memory of Elias Clayton, Elmer Jackson, and Isaac McGhie, as well as the countless others who endured the brutality of the African Dodger game or the indifference of the circus industry, urges us to confront the painful history of racial violence and exploitation in America. Remembering their lives—and the inhumane treatment they suffered—calls upon us to acknowledge the past's injustices and to reject the dehumanizing narratives that allowed such atrocities to occur. Their deaths demand a commitment to building a society where every life is valued, where no one is treated as a disposable object for profit or entertainment, and where justice, dignity, and equality are fundamental rights for all.

Segregation within the circus was easily enforced, with Black workers traveling in separate train cars and relegated to tasks that kept them behind the scenes, away from the audience's view. Though the circus promoted an image of inclusivity and joy, the reality for Black workers was one of grueling, thankless labor under conditions that barely recognized their humanity. This environment allowed the deeply ingrained racial prejudices of the time to flourish unchecked, reinforcing the notion that Black lives were less valuable than those of animals.

The vulnerability of Black circus workers became tragically evident on June 15, 1920, in Duluth, Minnesota. As part of the John Robinson Circus, three young Black men—barely out of their teens—were falsely accused of a crime and subsequently dragged from their beds, beaten, and lynched in a brutal public spectacle. Their bodies were hung from a wooden telegraph pole against the backdrop of the Shrine Temple and the Duluth cityscape. The local press referred to the scene as a "necktie party," and the mob even took photographs, immortalizing the horror and reinforcing the message of white supremacy.

The lynching of these young men shattered any illusions that the North was free from the racial violence often associated with the South. Despite Duluth's northern location, just below the Canadian border, this horrific event exposed the racial hatred and prejudice deeply embedded in American society. For the Black circus workers, their journey north may have held the hope of escaping the overt racial violence of the South, yet they found themselves facing the same prejudice, brutality, and injustice they had hoped to leave behind.

Each year, the John Robinson Circus traveled from town to town, bringing joy and excitement to the communities it visited. But for the Black workers who traveled with the circus, the reality was one of backbreaking work, low pay, and constant racial hostility. Townspeople eagerly anticipated the circus's arrival, yet few considered the grueling lives of the Black men who made the performances possible. The audiences saw only the polished spectacle, unaware of the exploitation and danger lurking behind the scenes.

The events of that June evening in Duluth not only revealed the extreme vulnerability of Black lives but also exposed the circus industry's disregard for their Black laborers. The same society that mourned the deaths of fourteen horses in a train wreck and callously deemed Black lives inferior was quick to ignore or even participate in a "necktie party" that ended the lives of three innocent young men. This lynching underscored the reality that, to many in the circus world and beyond, Black lives were seen as expendable, disposable, and undeserving of dignity or respect.

HORSES BETTER THAN NEGROES.

Amusing Exclamation of a Circus Manager Whose Train Was Wrecked.

DUBUQUE, Iowa, July 8.—*Special Telegram.*—Cook & Whitby's circus train of twenty-two cars, en route from Prairie du Chien, Wis., to Maquoketa, Iowa, was passing Sny Magill, six miles below McGregor, at 2:45 o'clock this morning, when a defective axle caused the forward truck of the first car to break. Five cars were ditched and thirty horses killed. In a car with fourteen horses were a band of colored musicians. Every horse in the car was killed outright, but all the negroes escaped except two, one of whom was hurt dangerously, the other not seriously. The loss falls upon the circus managers, as the train was running not faster than ten miles an hour and on a straight track. It will ruin the circus, and the manager, realizing this, rushed about the wreck with tears in his eyes, shouting: "Just think of it! My fourteen best horses killed and every one of these darkies saved!"

The Inter Ocean Newspaper, Chicago, Illinois, Saturday, July 9, 1892, Article: "Horses Better Than Negroes."

This dark chapter in Duluth's history challenges future generations to confront the painful legacy of racial injustice. It is a reminder of the human cost behind the circus' shimmering veneer and the racial violence that was, and sometimes remains, ingrained in American society. The memory of the young men lynched in Duluth serves as both a somber testament to the past and a call to recognize the humanity of those once deemed expendable. It urges us to understand that the devaluation of any life degrades us all and that the fight for justice and equality requires a relentless commitment to honoring the worth and dignity of every individual.

The African Dodger Game

The African Dodger game, a grotesque form of entertainment in early 20th-century circuses and carnivals, was a public display of brutality masked as amusement. For the price of five cents, carnival-goers could buy the opportunity to hurl a baseball at the face of a Black man, who was forced to stick his head through a hole and endure the blows. These Black men, called "Dodgers," had no chance to avoid the balls, despite the name of the game. They were required to keep their heads exposed, knowing that every throw brought them closer to serious injury. For many, this cruel spectacle left permanent marks on their bodies and spirits, as fractured jaws, shattered noses, and damaged eyes were common outcomes of their repeated exposure to this violence. However, for the crowds that gathered to participate, these injuries were simply part of the spectacle, a source of added excitement for those who saw the Dodger's pain as part of the price of admission.

The injuries sustained by these men were severe, yet they received no medical treatment, no compensation, and no care from those who organized or profited from the game. Instead, these Black men were left to endure their suffering in silence, often without the means to recover properly. The scant payment they received for their participation in the game was a fraction of the carnival's profits, and it did not even begin to cover the costs—physical, emotional, or financial—of the injuries they sustained. Many "Dodgers" were permanently disfigured, their lives irrevocably altered for the brief amusement of a crowd that saw them as less than human.

The newspaper articles that covered their injuries often did so with a sense of detachment, if not outright amusement. Rather than sparking outrage or sympathy, these reports were presented as another form of entertainment for those who might have missed the event. The coverage reinforced the public's view of these men as objects of ridicule rather than individuals deserving of dignity and care. This practice revealed a profound cultural indifference to the bodily harm inflicted on Black men for entertainment, treating their suffering as something to be trivialized or ignored.

The African Dodger game was emblematic of the broader dehumanization that Black men faced in the circus industry. Black roustabouts, who were relegated to the hardest, dirtiest, and most dangerous jobs within the circus, were similarly seen as expendable labor. Paid less than their white counterparts and kept segregated in separate train cars, these men were expected to carry out backbreaking work under grueling conditions, all while facing daily racial hostility. The circus management viewed their Black laborers as little more than tools, essential to the circus's operations but entirely disposable. Their lives were treated with the same disregard as those of the African Dodgers—both groups were exploited, mistreated, and offered no medical care for their injuries.

This broader culture of dehumanization and disregard reached its apex in the lynching of Elias Clayton, Elmer Jackson, and Isaac McGhie in Duluth on June 15, 1920. These young Black men, who traveled north with the John Robinson Circus, may have hoped that life in the Midwest would offer a respite from the dangers they knew in the South. However, when a young white woman falsely accused Black men from the circus of assault, the pervasive racial hostility that simmered beneath the surface of northern society erupted into a violent lynching. Without evidence or trial, Clayton, Jackson, and McGhie were jailed, then brutally taken by a mob of thousands who stormed the police station, determined to exact their own form of "justice."

The lynching of these men was a grotesque public spectacle, eerily reminiscent of the African Dodger game in its callous disregard for Black lives. The crowd beat, tortured, and hung them from a telegraph pole in the middle of Duluth, transforming the event into a perverse form of communal entertainment. As with the African Dodger game, injuries were inflicted without care or concern, and the men's suffering was treated as a sideshow for the amusement of the mob. Photographs were taken of the hanging bodies, and these images were later printed as postcards and sold, reinforcing the culture that saw Black pain and death as consumable commodities.

For Black circus workers like Clayton, Jackson, and McGhie, the constant travel from one town to the next offered little protection from the racial hatred that permeated American society. They knew that their lives were precarious, that at any moment, a baseless accusation or violent whim could lead to their deaths. Their work for the circus, though essential, afforded them no safety, no stability, and no defense against the mob's brutal, racist violence. The tragedy in Duluth made it painfully clear that even in the supposedly progressive North, Black men's lives were viewed as expendable.

The events in Duluth exposed the harsh truth that Black people in America were often seen not as human beings but as targets for white anger, tools for white profit, and objects for white entertainment. The lynching, like the African Dodger game and the disregard shown for injured Black roustabouts, underscored a society willing to exploit and harm Black individuals without consequence. The systemic failure to protect, treat, or value these lives reflected the broader, entrenched racism that governed American life.

This legacy continues to challenge us today. The memory of Elias Clayton, Elmer Jackson, and Isaac McGhie, as well as the countless others who endured the brutality of the African Dodger game or the indifference of the circus industry, urges us to confront the painful history of racial violence and exploitation in America. Remembering their lives—and the inhumane treatment they suffered—calls upon us to acknowledge the past's injustices and to reject the dehumanizing narratives that allowed such atrocities to occur. Their deaths demand a commitment to building a society where every life is valued, where no one is treated as a disposable object for profit or entertainment, and where justice, dignity, and equality are fundamental rights for all.

THE ACCUSATION:

The lynchings in Duluth began with a lie, rooted in the intersecting fears and racial biases of the era. Irene Tusken, a young white girl, and her boyfriend, James Sullivan, had gone to a secluded ravine near the circus grounds to escape the prying eyes of her parents. Tusken's parents disapproved of her relationship with Sullivan, who, as Michael Fedo details in The Lynchings in Duluth, was a brash young man with little regard for authority or consequence. The young couple's dalliance in the woods left Tusken's clothing dirty, and rather than admit their actions to her family, Sullivan manufactured a story to explain her disheveled appearance.

He claimed that Tusken had been assaulted by Black men from the nearby circus.

Duluth's residents were ready to accept this story without question. In the racial climate of the time, an accusation against Black men was enough to spark immediate outrage. "Now, it can't be certain the offense needed to be more severe than a supposed whistle to start this violence against innocent Black men because this hunger for revenge seemed to be brimming in Duluth for a long time," Fedo reflects. This observation captures the underlying tension in Duluth—resentment and racial hostility simmered just beneath the surface, waiting for a spark to ignite it. In this context, Sullivan's accusation was not merely accepted; it was welcomed.

Acting on this accusation, authorities quickly intercepted the circus train, which had already begun leaving Duluth. They forcibly removed nearly forty Black men from the train, pulling them aside for questioning. Among them, fourteen were detained, while seven were later released. The remaining six—Elias Clayton, Elmer Jackson, Nate Green, Loney Williams, John Thomas, and Isaac McGhie—were kept in custody. McGhie, a material witness rather than a suspect, was held under the presumption that his presence could help resolve the case. Despite the lack of evidence linking these men to any crime, Duluth's police chief found something "off" in their statements, justifying their continued detention. Meanwhile, officers drove to Virginia, Minnesota, hoping to detain more Black circus workers to strengthen their case, a desperate attempt to placate a volatile public with "suspects."

Medical examinations of Tusken provided no evidence of assault, but this did nothing to quell the mounting anger. Once the accusation was made, it took on a life of its own, feeding the crowd's desire for retribution. This atmosphere of anger and fear quickly spread through Duluth, uniting the community around a lie. And for the men in custody, the baseless accusation was enough to turn the city against them.

THE RIOT:

By nightfall, the mob had gathered, fueled by the growing belief in the accusation and a collective desire for vengeance. As word of the alleged assault circulated, a crowd began forming outside the Duluth police station. Fedo describes a scene that quickly escalated into chaos: by the time the mob was fully assembled, nearly 10,000 people filled the streets, each one agitated by the others around them. What had started as scattered conversations and murmurs quickly evolved into chants, threats, and, eventually, violence. For Duluth's white residents, this accusation was more than just a single event—it was an opportunity to assert power, enforce racial hierarchy, and send a message to the Black community.

William Henry Ray, a Black man who had recently moved to Duluth from the South, was working his usual shift at the ore docks on the bayfront that night. When Ray heard about the accusation, his mind raced to the stories he knew too well: stories of Black men who were lynched in the South on the slightest pretext or unfounded rumors. Though he had come north hoping to escape the pervasive violence of his youth, Ray felt a chilling familiarity in the rumors swirling around him. He knew that this accusation alone could be a death sentence for any Black men the mob might seize.

As the crowd outside the police station grew, it became clear that law enforcement was unprepared, and perhaps unwilling, to protect the men in their custody. Police Chief John Murphy, along with several officers, had already left for Virginia, Minnesota, chasing vague leads. This decision left the jail minimally guarded, a fact that the crowd quickly took advantage of. They battered down the doors, overpowered the few officers inside, and seized three of the six men held in custody—Clayton, Jackson, and McGhie. The mob's anger was laser-focused, sparing the remaining men as they dragged Clayton, Jackson, and McGhie out onto the streets.

The three young men were brutalized as they were paraded through Duluth's downtown streets. Their bodies were beaten, their clothes torn, and their faces bloodied, all while the mob hurled racial slurs and insults. This violence was not random; it was calculated, intended to demean and degrade the men, to strip them of their humanity before what was to come. For the mob, this was more than punishment—it was a twisted form of communal entertainment. The violence fed itself, each blow and insult stoking the fury of the crowd as they prepared for the ultimate act of brutality.

THE LYNCHING:

The mob dragged Clayton, Jackson, and McGhie to a wooden telegraph pole near the Shrine Temple, a location chosen for its prominence in Duluth's cityscape. Here, in a highly visible and public space, the crowd hanged the three young men, transforming their deaths into a spectacle. This was not just a killing; it was an assertion of power, a message to every Black resident of Duluth that they were vulnerable, disposable, and unwelcome. Fedo recounts how some in the mob took photographs of the men's lifeless bodies, later printing these images on postcards that were sold as souvenirs. These postcards reduced the men's suffering to a collectible, a grotesque memento that underscored the normalization of violence against Black people.

The following morning, when William Henry Ray's shift ended, he walked through the streets of downtown Duluth, dreading what he might find. His worst fears were realized when he saw the bodies of Clayton, Jackson, and McGhie lying on the ground, where they had been left after being cut down from the pole. For Ray, this sight was both a horrifying confirmation of his worst fears and a brutal reminder of the violence he thought he had left behind in the South. The lynching made it painfully clear that racial hatred knew no geographic boundaries; it thrived just as strongly in the North as in the South.

As Ray looked upon the bodies, he was struck not only by the brutality of the lynching but by the indifference of the community around him. White passersby hurried past, averting their eyes, unwilling to acknowledge the horror before them. Ray later described this silence as almost as disturbing as the violence itself. For him, the lynching was not just an isolated event—it was a public assertion of racial hierarchy, a warning that no Black life in Duluth was safe.

In Fedo's recounting, Ray's experience serves as a profound commentary on the culture of racial violence that permeated America. The events of that night in Duluth were not simply a response to an alleged crime; they were a manifestation of the systemic racism that devalued Black lives, allowing communities to act with impunity. The lynching of Clayton, Jackson, and McGhie revealed the depths of hatred that lay beneath the surface of American society, turning a lie into a death sentence with terrifying ease. For Duluth's Black residents, the lynching shattered any illusion of safety, underscoring the harsh reality that no amount of distance from the South could shield them from the racial violence endemic to the nation.

The legacy of that night, preserved in photographs and the accounts of survivors like Ray, stands as a stark reminder of the power of hatred and the ease with which communities could abandon justice in favor of vengeance. The events in Duluth challenged future generations to confront the dark history of racial violence, to remember the lives lost, and to commit to a world where no person is targeted, dehumanized, or erased because of the color of their skin. The lynching of Elias Clayton, Elmer Jackson, and Isaac McGhie remains a painful testament to the enduring scars of racism in America, a call to remember and to change.

NEWS COVERAGE:

The word in Minnesota seemed not to fully align. Some newspapers labeled the event a disgrace and a stain on the town of Duluth. Others stated the Negro men were just like dogs and the only reasonable thing to do was to "put them down."

Despite the absence of proof against the lynched men, despite the strong indication that the story of assault was a fabrication, to the contrary, the press of the country gave a wilder and more prominent display of these statements. The press promoted the narrative that Black men had attacked a white girl beyond a reasonable doubt. This narrative caused the bestiality and mobbish that rang through the streets of Duluth. There was no attempt on the part of the press to correct the viciously misleading impression that had gone forth to the country. The New York Times carried an article with a single statement indicating that Chief of Police John Murphy had proven at least one of the men innocents. The rest of the article was still laced with falsehoods and significant exaggerations about what had transpired. But one had to ask, had they been charged? They were just taken off the train and detained—but did not make it through the night.

Three lynched African American men (two hanging from a post, one laying on the ground) surrounded by a crowd of witnesses (Library of Congress Online Catalog 1,584,677)
https://www.loc.gov/resource/cph.3a35788/

PICTURES OF LYNCHING SELL FOR 50 CENTS EACH

VIRGINIA, June 18.—Pictures of the Duluth lynching showing two bodies still hanging to the light post and one on the ground, made their appearance in Virginia today and found ready customers at 50 cents each.

https://www.tptoriginals.org/100-years-after-the-duluth-lynching-another-face-is-added-to-the-mob-of-systemic-racism

SATURDAY, JUNE 19, 1920

MINNESOTA'S DISGRACE.

The disgraceful carnal assault on a female and the disgraceful execution of mob vengeance on three men at Duluth, Minnesota, has been told so generally in the daily papers everywhere that no detailed account needs to be made by THE APPEAL.

But with the rest of the fair-minded papers and people we wish to add our condemnation of the crime of assault as perpetrated and also the murderous spirit of the mob. We cannot find words to express our utter horror of either or both, but will allow the sentiments expressed by others, with which we are in hearty accord, to in a measure do that for us.

The St. Paul Daily News said:

"That the three men were charged with the vilest of crimes is no justification for 'lynch law.' Had they been guilty, there is no doubt that proof, conviction and punishment would have followed swiftly—BUT—under due process of law.

"Minnesota's Disgrace" by Editor
The Appeal St. Paul, Minnesota,
June 19, 1920

A WITNESS

In a world where every facet of life was shaped by the color of one's skin, passing as white offered Oscar an escape from the brutal realities faced by Black men in America. But by choosing to live as a white man, Oscar, Ethel's brother, was also making a profound decision to deny his Black heritage, distancing himself from his own community, and from a lineage that carried both strength and struggle. The choice to pass as white wasn't merely a way to avoid discrimination; it required a constant suppression of his identity, a concealment of the truth of who he was and where he came from.

For Oscar, this decision offered access to a life that might otherwise be denied to him. Passing as white opened doors to social spaces, shielding him from the relentless prejudice faced by Black men. It allowed him a degree of freedom from the humiliations and hostilities that marked Black life in America. But this choice came at a cost—an ongoing act of self-erasure that kept him constantly alert, carefully guarding his words, actions, and associations to avoid exposure.

Oscar was working at a shoe shop in downtown Duluth that fateful night when he was engulfed with the mob. He believed he could continue moving unnoticed, blending into the shadows. But stepping outside, he was suddenly caught in a mob of white Duluthians surging through the streets, chanting, "Get the niggers!" The anger in their voices chilled him, but he dared not show his fear. He knew the danger of standing out, of failing to appear as just another white face in the crowd. Pushed along by the mob, he found himself swept to the corner of Second Avenue and Superior Street, where three Black men were being dragged through the streets, stripped, and savagely beaten by the crowd.

As the young men were strung up on the telegraph pole amid the mob's cheers, Oscar felt a surge of anger. But instead of acting on it, he instinctively shouted along with the crowd, chanting, "Lynch him! Lynch him!" His light skin, in that moment, felt like a fragile shield against the hatred around him, protecting him by allowing him to pass as one of the mob. He felt a temporary, twisted safety in that disguise, only to realize how hollow it was when he locked eyes with Adolph Juten—a known KKK member who had gone to school with Oscar and knew his true background. In Adolph's piercing gaze, Oscar saw the truth: his protection was an illusion, and if Adolph chose to expose him, he would become the mob's next target.

Fear flooded through him, and Oscar turned and ran, heart pounding, leaving the scene behind. He had narrowly escaped the violence, yet he could not escape the deep sense of shame that gripped him. In denying his Black heritage, he had saved himself—but he had also joined in the chants, blended into the hatred, and momentarily betrayed his own people.

That night forced Oscar to confront the painful duality of his existence. By denying his Black heritage, he had sought refuge in a world that would never truly accept him. He had erased his identity to protect himself, but in doing so, he had distanced himself from the community that shared his struggles and from the history he carried within him. Passing as white had afforded him certain protections, but at the cost of hiding his heritage and severing ties to his own roots. The sight of the young men hanging from the post haunted him, a reminder of the price he paid to remain safe—and of the reality he would carry with him for the rest of his life.

THE BLACK GRAPEVINE

In Duluth, as in many communities, the Black community relied on an informal, yet deeply trusted network of communication often referred to as the "Black grapevine." This grassroots network was essential for sharing news, warnings, and critical information during times when mainstream sources often neglect or distort issues affecting Black people. With widespread mistrust in white-run newspapers and institutions, the grapevine became served as a lifeline, enabling the community to stay informed and protect themselves amid pervasive hostility.

The grapevine was not only about relaying facts but about communicating the emotional gravity of events. When word of the lynchings spread, Duluth's Black residents learned the grim details through the grapevine. Friends, family, and neighbors shared whispered accounts, many fearful yet unable to ignore the horror. Each person who passed along the news did so with a heavy heart, painfully aware that the lives of three young Black men—Elias Clayton, Elmer Jackson, and Isaac McGhie—had been brutally ended in a public display of racial hatred.

Elders shared stories and warnings, reminding younger generations of similar events across the country, underscoring that the North, like the South, was rife with racial hostility. The grapevine spread messages of resilience, urging residents to remain vigilant, avoid confrontations, and care for one another. It became a channel for both collective grieving and mutual support, allowing the Black community to process their shared trauma and prepare for what might come next. Even in the darkest moments, the grapevine served as a powerful source of solidarity, keeping Duluth's Black community connected and informed amid pervasive threats.

The lynching's impact was devastating, sparking waves of shock, grief, anger, and fear. The community reacted with a profound sense of vulnerability, painfully aware that what had happened to Clayton, Jackson, and McGhie could easily happen to any one of them. Upon hearing the news, many retreated into their homes, seeking solace with family and trusteed neighbors, where they felt safer from public hostility. Families gathered close, warning their children to avoid the streets. For parents, the tragedy necessitated painful conversations with their children about resilience and caution in a world that devalued Black lives.

In the wake of the lynching, some members of Duluth's Black community reached out to local Black churches and civic organizations to discuss ways to protect one another and honor the lives of the three young men. Churches became spaces of refuge, where congregants gathered to pray and to draw strength. Pastors offered words of solace and resilience, emphasizing the need for unity. Some community members also began working to engage sympathetic white allies and leaders, hoping to build coalitions to prevent future violence. These efforts underscored the community's resilience and determination to seek safety and justice, even in a city that had shown them unimaginable hostility.

The tragedy forced a sobering realization: their lives were in constant jeopardy, demanding caution in their daily lives. Some began planning to leave Duluth altogether, realizing the North was not the safe haven they once imagined. Others resolved to stay but became more reserved, careful to avoid drawing unwanted attention. Every interaction now carried a sense of fear and distrust, as Duluth's social fabric felt irrevocably torn.

In the days and weeks that followed, the Black community in Duluth moved forward with a renewed sense of purpose, navigating fear and heartbreak. They mourned, they warned each other, they protected their own, and, above all, they resolved to survive. This commitment to survival in the face of terror became a testament to their resilience, underscoring the power of unity during hardship and leaving a legacy of courage and solidarity.

William Henry Ray and the Formation of the Duluth NAACP

In the wake of the lynchings, William Henry Ray, Ethel's father, emerged as a key figure in the push for change, serving as the impetus behind establishing the Duluth chapter of the NAACP. Ray's resolve to address the systemic racism and violence that led to the lynchings became a driving force, as he saw the need for an organized effort to fight for justice, equality, and protection for Black citizens.

Ray's determination inspired others in the community to join him, recognizing that change would require not only resilience but a unified voice. The formation of the NAACP chapter provided a platform for advocating accountability, pushing back against racial injustices, and honoring the memories of Elias Clayton, Elmer Jackson, and Isaac McGhie. This chapter became both a symbol of resistance and a beacon of hope, marking a pivotal moment in Duluth's history and laying the groundwork for ongoing efforts to confront and combat racial discrimination in the North.

CHAPTER 4: SEVERANCE

Throughout high school, Ethel's brother Will worked a range of jobs, from driving for Cox Brothers Provision Co. in 1907, to working as a mailer for the Evening Herald newspaper in 1908, and later as a clerk in 1910. Yet, despite his hard work, Will felt the weight of his heritage pressing down on his ambitions. Staying in Duluth meant he would always be seen as the son of a Black man. He believed that to become something greater, he needed to distance himself from the painful legacy that bound him to his father's identity—and ultimately pass as a white man.

One day, Will found a novel in his father's library: The House Behind the Cedars by Charles W. Chesnutt. This 1900 book tells the story of John and Rena Warwick, light-skinned siblings of mixed ancestry who leave their childhood home in North Carolina to begin new lives in South Carolina, passing as white. John finds success as a lawyer and even marries a white woman, building a life where he feels accepted and accomplished. But when he asks his sister, Rena, to help raise his son, her presence reawakens the tension between their identities. Rena falls in love with George Tyson, a business associate of John's, who, unaware of her heritage, asks her to marry him. Yet, as the relationship deepens, so does Rena's fear of exposure. When George discovers her true background, he breaks off their engagement, shattering the lives they had both hoped to build. This exposure ultimately costs both siblings their new lives and dreams.

Will saw himself in John and Rena, understanding the risks and fears of passing. He knew that to embrace a new identity, he would have to leave Duluth behind. Working for the railroad became his way out, offering him the means to escape and distance himself from a community that knew him too well. On the railroad, he found a sense of purpose and camaraderie with his fellow workers, who shared a similar drive for freedom and opportunity. This work also connected him to a community he could safely belong to, granting him social connection without the fear of exposure. The railroad industry in 1909 was thriving in Portland, Oregon, where the Northern Pacific Railroad offered numerous opportunities for those willing to work hard—train conductors, brakemen, engineers, telegraph operators, and more. It was a chance for Will to build a future far from the constraints of his past.

With enough savings, Will bought a ticket on the Northern Pacific Railroad to Portland, hoping that Oregon would offer him the fresh start he longed for. At just eighteen, he left home, moving into a modest room behind 355 Flanders Street in Portland. He took a job as a waiter, a stepping stone to further opportunities. Will's journey was about more than physical distance; it was an act of severance, a path to create a new identity, one where he could pass as white and, perhaps, find the acceptance and success he had only dreamed of in Duluth.

The decision for a Black person to pass as white in early 20th-century America was complex, fraught with both practical and deeply personal implications. Passing was not merely an act of altering one's physical appearance; it was a profound transformation that demanded a complete reimagining of one's identity and a severing of connections to family, heritage, and community. For Black individuals like Will, passing as white offered the allure of freedom from the racial limitations imposed by society. It opened doors to jobs, education, social acceptance, and safety from the constant threat of violence or discrimination. Yet, these opportunities came with high emotional and social costs, creating a life shaped by secrecy, loneliness, and the perpetual fear of exposure.

The act of passing placed individuals in a world where they could not fully claim their origins. They had to carefully avoid any association with their Black heritage, which meant distancing themselves from family members, friends, and cultural traditions that might hint at their true background. For many, this severance from their roots was deeply painful. Every interaction required vigilance to avoid slip-ups—any conversation, photograph, or hint of family history could give them away. Their relationships became inherently limited; even those closest to them would never fully know who they truly were, as sharing their past could compromise their constructed identity.

Psychologically, passing demanded a constant balancing act between the security it afforded and the shame or guilt that accompanied the denial of one's heritage. For some, passing led to feelings of self-betrayal. They were, after all, adopting an identity that society deemed superior, and in doing so, they risked internalizing the very prejudices that had oppressed them. This internal conflict often fostered feelings of isolation, as they lived in spaces where they could never be fully authentic or open. Many feared the repercussions of being discovered, which could range from social ostracism to violent retaliation.

The societal expectations around race further complicated passing. In a world deeply invested in racial hierarchies, any ambiguity was suspicious. Light-skinned Black individuals were often subjected to scrutiny from white peers suspicious of their "background," and from Black peers who felt that passing was a betrayal of solidarity. The wider Black community viewed passing with a mixture of empathy and ambivalence, understanding the pressures that led some to choose this path while also seeing it as a rejection of shared struggles and achievements.

For Will, passing as white was not merely an escape from racial prejudice; it was a means to reinvent himself in a world where he could access opportunities previously denied to him. His choice represented a deep conflict: in seeking freedom and opportunity, he had to reject his heritage, embracing a new identity at the cost of severing ties to his family and community. By stepping into a white identity, he would also absorb the privileges and complexities that came with it. The decision to pass, then, was not a straightforward one—it was layered with personal sacrifice, moral ambiguity, and the ever-present risk of losing both the new identity he had constructed and the roots that had once defined him.

MARITAL CLOAKS

After moving to Portland, Oregon, Will made his living working on the railroad and as a waiter, roles that allowed him to build a stable life away from his Duluth roots. By the time he was twenty-three, he was working as a concrete worker in Pendleton, Oregon, where he met Mary Welch, a strikingly beautiful woman with olive skin and dark features. Though Mary was thirty-eight, her youthful appearance belied her age, and she quickly captivated Will. Early in their courtship, Mary confided in him that she was "Colored," a revelation that allowed Will to admit his own Black heritage, a secret he closely guarded. With this shared understanding, they bonded quickly, and the two were married in 1912 in Vancouver, Washington. Mary explained that she had been married twice before, with no children, and was now divorced and widowed.

World War I erupted in 1914, but Will chose not to enlist, preferring to stay in Oregon to protect his wife. However, as time passed, he noticed that Mary began disappearing for days without explanation. His mind raced with possibilities, fearing that her secret identity as a Black woman passing as white might have been discovered, forcing her into a compromising situation. Despite these worries, he resisted the idea that she was being unfaithful. In 1917, when she urged him to enlist in the draft, he took the opportunity to question her absences. Reluctantly, Mary revealed a hidden life more complex than he could have imagined.

Mary Welch was born Mary Smith in 1871, not 1874 as she'd claimed. She presented Will with a box of documents revealing multiple identities: adoption papers, marriage certificates, and various forms of identification. Among these, Will found a certificate verifying Mary's Native American heritage. Far from being "Colored" as she had told him, Mary had been living on an Indian reservation when they met, receiving tribal compensation throughout their marriage. When he questioned her further, asking if she was still married to someone else, Mary took offense, gathered her belongings, and left without a word. Will never to see her again.

Mary's decision to tell Will she was Black rather than admit she was Native American speaks to the complex dynamics of identity and survival in a society where racial classifications carried distinct social consequences. In early 20th-century America, racial hierarchies were rigidly enforced, but they were also influenced by specific regional and social perceptions. For Mary, passing as Black rather than Native American may have been a pragmatic choice rooted in both personal safety and societal dynamics.

First, identifying as Black could have offered Mary a clearer path to stability within certain social circles. While both Black and Native American communities faced significant discrimination, the avenues to assimilate into mainstream society were often different. Many Native Americans faced forced assimilation policies, including the reservation system, boarding schools, and restricted movement and employment. By passing as Black, Mary could have distanced herself from these constraints, aligning herself with an identity that, while still marginalized, was not subject to the same mechanisms of control.

At thirty-eight, she wasn't considered young by early 20th-century standards, and age was closely tied to perceptions of a woman's vitality and worth. Presenting herself as younger allowed Mary to align herself with a version of herself that felt more fitting for a fresh start. Youth made her more appealing in marriage, socially adaptable, and unburdened by the complexities that might have made her seem less trustworthy or desirable.

Similarly, erasing her previous marriages and children from her story was a way to shed associations with past obligations that could complicate her future. Twice married and with children, Mary may have worried that she'd be labeled as a woman with "baggage," carrying societal stigmas that might limit her options. In that era, a divorced or widowed mother was often viewed differently, seen as carrying social or economic burdens. By omitting her children from her narrative, Mary could present herself as unencumbered and free, rather than as a woman tied to previous roles and responsibilities. Reinventing her identity allowed her to gain control over how others perceived her, freeing her from expectations tied to motherhood and marital history.

Not admitting she had lived on a reservation was another significant decision. Reservation life was often associated with limited rights, poverty, and forced assimilation policies, and for Native Americans, it carried restrictive and social implications. By omitting her connection to reservation life, Mary could distance herself from stereotypes and biases that may have negatively influenced how people viewed her. This was especially important in an environment where Native Americans were often treated as outsiders. Mary's choice to present herself as "Colored" and separate from reservation roots allowed her to forge a broader social standing, avoiding the hostility or prejudice frequently directed at Native American communities.

In constructing this new identity, Mary sought agency and protection in a world that would judge her harshly based on her actual history. Her lies were survival mechanisms in a society with rigid categories and biases, and they reflect the lengths individuals often went to secure dignity, acceptance, and control over their lives. For Mary, reinventing her age, family, and background allowed her a degree of freedom that her identity might not have afforded. Her choices underscore how profoundly individuals were affected by societal biases, and the measures they took to find their place amid these pressures.

Moreover, the burgeoning Black communities of the time had developed support networks, particularly in urban areas. Churches, fraternal organizations, and social clubs provided a sense of community and protection that would have been accessible to Mary under a Black identity. By identifying as Black, Mary might have been able to access these networks and find camaraderie, resources, and a certain level of stability unavailable to her as a Native American woman, especially if she lived in predominantly Black neighborhoods or worked in places where these affiliations were assumed.

Mary's decision might also have been shaped by personal relationships and individual survival strategies. She may have felt safer revealing a shared "Colored" identity to Will, knowing it would create a bond and understanding between them. If Mary had experienced mistreatment or prejudice due to her Native American background, she might have perceived identifying as Black to shield herself from both her past and the complexities that came with her Native identity, while also gaining a sense of control over how she was perceived.

Finally, by framing herself as Black rather than Native American, Mary could present a narrative that perhaps resonated with Will's own struggles around race and identity. In early 20th-century America, where racial boundaries were heavily policed, each racial identity came with specific cultural and legal expectations. Mary may have understood that claiming a shared Black identity with Will could forge a stronger, more intimate connection while also easing any fears he might have had about her being "outed" in predominantly white spaces. This complex decision to pass within a particular racial framework reflected her need for protection, connection, and stability, even if it ultimately meant concealing parts of her heritage.

In this way, Mary's choice to pass as Black rather than Native American wasn't simply about deception; it reflected the survival strategies required in a world where any hint of difference could lead to discrimination or even danger. It speaks of the difficult choices individuals like Mary had to make to navigate their lives within a system that constantly sought to categorize and marginalize them.

Disillusioned and seeking a fresh start, Will returned to Duluth briefly, reconnecting with his sister, Ethel, and the family he had left behind. The war draft was underway, and both he and his brother Oscar enlisted, feeling both a sense of duty and the weight of opportunity that military service could bring. Will's return brought mixed emotions for Ethel. She had long yearned to leave Duluth, to break free from the prejudices and limitations of their hometown, but Will urged her to wait until he returned from service. He had promised they would plan together, giving her hope that he would help her escape the stifling environment that kept her aspirations caged. With his encouragement, Ethel threw herself into applying for stenographer positions across the country, eagerly anticipating the chance to move, to step into a world beyond the boundaries of Duluth.

While Ethel held onto her dreams of leaving, Will was already considering a different path, one that led him further from his roots. Although his first marriage had ended painfully, he eventually remarried in Portland, this time to Amanda Murphy, a white woman with a young son from a previous marriage. In 1923, they married, and their union allowed Will to construct a new identity, one that offered the safety and acceptance he had long sought but could never fully attain as a Black man. By marrying Amanda, Will could blend even more seamlessly into white society, shielded from the harsh realities he would face if he were open about his heritage. As a husband and stepfather, he was cloaked in the respectability and security that came with being seen as a white family man—a life that shielded him from the constant threat of racial discrimination but also distanced him from the family he had left behind.

For Ethel, Will's choices felt like a profound abandonment. She had waited, applied for jobs, and stayed in Duluth in the hope that he would be there to help her begin a new life. But in her journal, she wrote of her disappointment, lamenting his silence on the matter of her moving west. She couldn't help but feel that he had broken his promise, that he had chosen a life in which there was no room for her. Will's new life in Portland represented both his personal liberation and a painful separation from the family that had always been his anchor. As Ethel watched her brother embrace his role in a society that accepted him as white, she was left to grapple with the realization that he had chosen a path that separated him from the family and heritage they had once shared. The brother who had once protected her and assured her of a future together had now stepped into a life where his ties to his past—his ties to her—had all but faded away.

As the years passed, Will's life in Portland became a reminder of the costs of passing as white. For him, the choice had offered new possibilities, but it had also necessitated a distancing from his identity and history. For Ethel, it underscored the isolation she felt in Duluth and the loss of a sibling who had once been her closest ally. His departure and his transformation left her not only with a broken promise but also with a painful understanding of the sacrifices her brother had made—and the sacrifices he had left her to bear alone.

Ethel Ray, circa 1920

THE NEOPHYTE

In the aftermath of the 1920 Duluth lynchings, the Black community faced the daunting task of reclaiming their sense of safety and belonging in a city that had been shaken to its core. William Henry Ray, Ethel's father, recognized that action was needed to safeguard the community and renew faith in their right to live without fear. Together, William and Ethel took steps to reassure the community that they could remain in Duluth without the constant threat of violence. Yet, as this healing process began, a disturbing new chapter unfolded. In 1921, the Ku Klux Klan gained traction in Minnesota, setting its sights on the same city still reeling from racial terror.

The Klan, headquartered in Georgia, extended its reach northward, capitalizing on racial tensions and gathering support in Duluth. Klan members from Chicago and Minneapolis joined efforts to establish a local chapter in Duluth, recruiting from the local population. In August of that year, The Duluth Herald attempted to downplay the presence of the Klan, stating, "The great majority of the individuals in the Klan are men of good intentions, although narrow and without much vision...They do not know that one of the big things our ancestors fought for was doing away with autocratic power exercised by irresponsible tribunals." Despite these assurances, the Klan's influence grew rapidly. By the following year, the Duluth Klan chapter claimed over 1,500 members. In Minneapolis, North Star Klan No. 2 began regular meetings in local churches, drawing crowds across the state to Klan rallies and social gatherings.

MARCH 1921

Amid this rising tide of hate, Ethel Ray worked tirelessly between Duluth and the Twin Cities, striving to establish an NAACP chapter that could provide the Black community with both advocacy and a foundation for justice. Though the chapter was new and lacked resources, Ethel poured countless hours into its development, knowing it needed not only strength but also visibility beyond Duluth.

She was aware that W. E. B. Du Bois, a leading NAACP voice, would soon speak in the Twin Cities. Encouraged by her father, Ethel planned to attend and persuade Du Bois to visit Duluth to support their cause. She believed his presence could galvanize the community and draw much-needed attention to anti-lynching legislation in Minnesota. For Ethel, this was about more than securing a speaker; it was a chance to amplify the fight for justice and signal that Duluth's Black community would not be silenced. She hoped that Du Bois's words would rally public support for legislation to end the era of unchecked violence.

The Appeal, a St. Paul and Minneapolis newspaper, reported that Du Bois was visiting the Twin Cities to speak on the Pan-African Congress. The Duluth NAACP chapter, however, wanted him there to advocate for the Dyer Anti-Lynching legislation. Introduced in 1918 by Missouri Congressman Leonidas Dyer, the legislation sought to make lynching a federal felony punishable by imprisonment. Convincing Du Bois to speak in Duluth, a town recently scarred by lynching, was a difficult ask. Yet after some persuasion, he agreed, and Ethel accompanied him the 150 miles to Duluth the morning after his talk in Minneapolis at the People's Church. Ethel witnessed her father's admiration for Du Bois and understood why the community placed him on a pedestal. His clarity and humility marked him as a leader with a unique gift for communicating justice.

On March 21, 1921, Ethel introduced W. E. B. Du Bois at St. Marks AME Church:

"Good evening, ladies and gentlemen. I wish to pay special tribute to the splendid cooperation of the St. Paul and Minneapolis NAACP Branches in raising money for lawyers, reporters, and investigators of the Duluth lynching. Men perish, but their power goes on forever. As time goes on, we find that there is a deliverer bequeathed to every just cause…Our portion is, and yet will be, to drink a bitter cup. In many things, yet all must see, the race is moving up. Ladies and Gentlemen, look to the east from whence cometh all light; otherwise, darkness is intense. I take pleasure in introducing to you the rising son, Dr. W. E. B. Du Bois."

The church, with a capacity of 250, overflowed that night, with an audience three-fourths white -turnout that foreshadowed the widespread support the NAACP could harness in the years to come. The event marked a pivotal moment for the chapter, setting a high bar for its mission to fight for racial justice and equality.

THE KKK IN MINNESOTA

Ironically, Minnesota became the first state to pass an anti-lynching law in 1922, yet during this period, Klan activity surged. By 1923, approximately ten chapters operated in Minneapolis alone, with many emerging on college campuses throughout the Midwest, helping to swell the Klan's national membership to over 100,000. That same year, Minneapolis Mayor George Leach launched an investigation into possible Klan activity at the University of Minnesota after the Minnesota Daily reported suspicions of student Klan members. The Klan's influence persisted, and in 1925, they even secured a certificate of incorporation in Minnesota as a nonprofit organization.

LEAVING FOR A NEW OPPORTUNITY

On September 3, 1922, Ethel expressed her yearning for new opportunities, reflecting that "Duluth and Moose Lake couldn't hold her anymore." She felt ready for a greater calling in life. Although her position at the Minnesota Forest Fire Relief Commission provided a steady income, she had worked there for several years and knew it was time to move on. Mrs. Nellie Francis, a supportive figure whom Ethel regarded as a surrogate mother, encouraged her to apply for a position as a Legislative Clerk in the State capital. Ethel looked forward to the change, anticipating a new environment and the opportunity to immerse herself in the vibrant, supportive community of St. Paul and Minneapolis.

One month later, on October 4, Ethel's anticipation grew as she received the letter confirming her position with the Minnesota Legislature. She had secured a role as a stenographer and typist—the first Black woman to hold this position—earning $6 a week while serving on the Education, Apportionment, and Bank and Banking committees. Her term would last five months, from January to May 1923. Although temporary, the role opened doors to new connections and prospects, aligning her closer to her ultimate goal of working with a civic or social agency serving her community.

Through every step of her journey, Ethel remained committed to advocacy, driven by a desire for justice, and undeterred by the challenges that marked her path. Each milestone, from her groundbreaking work with the NAACP to her historic legislative role, was a testament to her resilience and to the community that supported her. She moved forward with a clear sense of purpose, knowing her story was part of a greater struggle for equality and dignity that would endure beyond her lifetime

Colored Girl Is Appointed Clerk In Legislature

Miss Ethel M. Ray of Duluth, daughter of Mr. and Mrs. W. H. Ray of Duluth, has been selected as one of the committee clerks in the legislature. Miss Ray is an efficient stenographer and typist, having served as stenographer two years during the settlement of the Moose Lake fire claims.

She was rated 100% for efficiency and courtesy upon inspection and has been assigned to three important committees. Several requests were made for her services. Miss Ray is an attractive young lady of very refined manners and a credit to her race.

Wednesday, December 13, 1922, *The Appeal*

In contrast to her brothers' path of passing, Ethel's journey was one of embracing her identity with unwavering resolve. Her mother, Inga, had chosen a difficult path of her own, marrying a Black man and raising a family in a world marked by rigid racial divides. Inga's life reflected resilience, compassion, and an unyielding commitment to her family and community. A white woman in an interracial marriage, Inga faced the prejudices of society alongside her husband, William Henry, but responded not with bitterness or fear, but with a deep-seated commitment to treating all people with dignity and respect. Her compassion reached beyond her family, touching the lives of those in her broader community who were also marginalized or in need. In a world fractured by racism, her life stood as a quiet but powerful testament to unity and empathy.

This influence, combined with William Henry's staunch belief in justice, became a guiding force for Ethel, shaping her values and her sense of self. Inga's compassion taught Ethel the importance of kindness, while William Henry's commitment to justice instilled in her the drive to confront wrongs and advocate for change. Their values lived on in her, giving her the foundation she needed to navigate the challenges that lay ahead. While her brothers sought safety in passing, Ethel recognized that her Blackness was not a barrier but a source of strength. She understood that her identity was more than a label; it was an inheritance of resilience, courage, and a call to action.

The loss of William Henry in November 1948, followed by Inga's passing just two months later, marked a profound shift in the Ray family. Ethel, already a woman of conviction, now felt the full weight of her family's legacy resting on her shoulders. Her father's death brought to light tensions that had long simmered within the family, particularly around the choices her brothers had made. In the months following his death, Ethel wrote a letter to her father, pouring out her frustrations and sense of betrayal regarding her brothers' decisions to live as white men. She recalled an exchange with Will, who had remarked, "You chose the right road—marrying colored was the right decision for you." Ethel responded with a mix of bitterness and pride. "Who is he to tell me what is right or wrong in my life?" she wrote, questioning the authority of a brother who had turned his back on his heritage.

In their mother's absence, Will confessed that he and Oscar finally felt a sense of "freedom," revealing the internalized shame and struggle that had defined their lives. This admission stirred a mix of clarity and sadness in Ethel, underscoring the different ways each sibling had processed the complexities of their identities. While her brothers had spent their lives evading the pain of racial discrimination, Ethel had embraced her heritage, finding purpose in her father's vision of justice.

William Henry's life had been guided by a commitment to justice that transcended personal safety. He saw it as his duty to fight not only for his own family but for all Black people who faced oppression. His journey from the South to Duluth in 1899, a region that would soon experience the horror of racial violence, only deepened his resolve. For him, survival was not enough—it required action and sacrifice. His life embodied the belief that dignity and progress came from standing up to injustice, regardless of the risks. This conviction became his legacy, one that Ethel would carry forward.

Ethel sometimes found her father's stance rigid, even frustrating, yet she respected his vision and the values he had instilled in her. His love for her, combined with his belief in justice, gave her the strength to pursue a life of advocacy and civil rights work. With his passing, Ethel took up his torch, determined to honor his legacy. Her work in activism and her steadfast commitment to her Black identity became a testament to the principles he had lived by. William Henry had taught her that true courage came from embracing one's identity and standing firm in the face of oppression—a lesson that became the foundation of her life's work.

This legacy of resilience and advocacy extended beyond Ethel to future generations. Her son, Glenn Ray Nance, took up the mantle, ensuring that the fight for justice would not end with her. Ethel's life and work provided a bridge between the past and the future, grounding her family's story in the pursuit of dignity and equality. Each generation took on the responsibility to carry forward these values, honoring the sacrifices and achievements of those who came before.

CHAPTER 5: A PRIVILEGE FOR A LIFE

Ethel's brothers, Oscar and Will, each made a profound decision to pass as white—a choice that reshaped their lives and set them on a path marked by secrecy, denial, and sacrifice. For both men, the decision to "pass" was not made lightly; it was a complex survival strategy in a society that saw their Blackness as an obstacle, a threat, something to be hidden if they wanted to advance. In the America of their time, passing as white was a ticket to the opportunities they craved but could never access as Black men. This choice, however, came with a painful cost, alienating them from their family and forcing them to sever ties with their past, their heritage, and even their true selves.

Oscar's decision to pass was driven by a relentless need for control and safety. Once he settled into his life as a white man, he guarded his identity with near-paranoid vigilance. When he later managed a store, he refused to hire Black employees, fearing that any association with Black people might expose his own hidden heritage. To him, the presence of Black workers was a risk, a reminder of the racial lineage he sought so desperately to erase. His fears ran so deep that he would rather exclude his own people from employment opportunities than risk the possibility of someone connecting him to the Black community.

Oscar's rejection of Blackness wasn't just about the desire for safety; it was a calculated attempt to erase himself from his own history. Each decision he made to distance himself from Black people was a small act of self-denial, an effort to construct a life where he could exist without fear of discovery. He convinced himself that proximity to Blackness would unravel the life he had built, that his performance as a white man would collapse, leaving him vulnerable. Oscar paid for his privilege by distancing himself from his roots and reshaping his identity to fit a world that would otherwise reject him. In doing so, he traded his heritage for a precarious sense of security, pushing his true self further and further into the shadows.

Will's path was different but equally fraught with complexities. He moved west to Oregon, where he carved out a life for himself as a white man. In his case, passing offered the chance to escape the prejudices and barriers that followed Black people in every aspect of life—where they could live, work, whom they could love, and whether they could be safe. Passing allowed him a life free from constant scrutiny and gave him access to opportunities he would never have had as an openly Black man. Yet, the decision isolated him from his family, friends, and community, severing him from his roots in a way that left lasting scars.

For Will, the choice to pass became a form of refuge, but it also became a prison. By hiding behind a white identity, he could evade the limitations imposed by society, but he could never truly escape the emotional toll. Every time he wrote letters home to his family, they were brief and guarded, as if he feared that even his words might betray him. His passing brought him safety but robbed him of belonging, forcing him into a life of solitude and internalized conflict. Will found a sense of peace hiding within the safety of his white family, yet he remained haunted by the sacrifices he had made to secure it. His white family became a shield, but it also marked the boundary between the life he lived and the life he had left behind.

Both brothers, in their way, followed the path their father had set, seeking a form of freedom from the constraints of their birth circumstances. William Henry had left the South, hoping to find safety and opportunity in Duluth, away from the racial violence and constraints that plagued Black families in the South. However, where William Henry chose to confront these struggles head-on, Oscar and Will saw freedom as something they could only achieve by escaping their identities. By leaving behind their family, heritage, and community, they thought they could access a different kind of liberation—a life untouched by racial prejudice.

Yet, in the eyes of those they left behind, their actions symbolized a betrayal, raising painful questions about what sacrifices are justifiable in the name of survival. Oscar and Will's choices reflected the painful duality of passing. On one hand, they gained access to a world they might otherwise have never known. On the other, they became strangers to their family and to themselves, existing in a shadowed space between acceptance and denial. Their actions forced those around them to confront difficult truths about survival and self-betrayal, and to question at what point survival itself becomes an abandonment of one's own identity.

In this context, Ethel stood as a counterpoint to her brothers' choices. She chose a different path, one that embraced her Black identity with pride and resilience. Where Oscar and Will sought security by blending in, Ethel chose to stand out, using her heritage as a source of strength and purpose. She recognized the courage and resilience embedded in her lineage and saw her identity not as a limitation, but as a foundation upon which she could build a life of meaning and advocacy. Ethel's choice to be openly and proudly Black, to embrace rather than reject her heritage, gave her life a sense of depth and integrity that her brothers' choices lacked.

Ethel's commitment to her Black identity became a cornerstone of her life. She viewed her heritage as a rich and empowering legacy, a source of inner strength and resilience that gave her the confidence to face the world without fear of rejection. Her activism, her advocacy, and her determination to fight for justice and equality towered over the anxieties that had driven her brothers away. Ethel's life became a testament to the power of self-acceptance, a reminder that true strength lies in embracing one's roots rather than denying them.

In the end, the choices of Oscar, Will, and Ethel reflected the complex, often heartbreaking ways that race and identity shaped the lives of Black people in early 20th-century America. Oscar and Will sought safety in a society that equated Blackness with danger and limitation, but their quest for security came at a profound personal cost. In their rejection of their heritage, they lost not only their family but also a part of themselves. Ethel, in choosing to embrace her identity fully, found a sense of purpose and strength that her brothers could never attain. Her life, filled with courage, conviction, and integrity, became a powerful rebuke to the fears and compromises that had defined her brothers' lives.

Through her, the Ray family's legacy found a new path, one grounded in pride, resilience, and an unwavering commitment to justice. Her choice to remain true to herself, even in a world that rejected her for it, became an act of defiance, a reminder of the power of authenticity in a society that demanded conformity. In Ethel, the family's legacy of bravery and dignity endured, finding its truest and most inspiring form.

CHAPTER 6: UNYIELDING TRUTH: A LEGACY OF IDENTITY AND RESOLVE

In contrast to her brothers' path of passing, Ethel's journey was one of embracing her identity with unwavering resolve. Her mother, Inga, had chosen a difficult path of her own, marrying a Black man and raising a family in a world marked by rigid racial divides. Inga's life reflected resilience, compassion, and an unyielding commitment to her family and community. A white woman in an interracial marriage, Inga faced the prejudices of society alongside her husband, William Henry, but responded not with bitterness or fear, but with a deep-seated commitment to treating all people with dignity and respect. Her compassion reached beyond her family, touching the lives of those in her broader community who were also marginalized or in need. In a world fractured by racism, her life stood as a quiet but powerful testament to unity and empathy.

This influence, combined with William Henry's staunch belief in justice, became a guiding force for Ethel, shaping her values and her sense of self. Inga's compassion taught Ethel the importance of kindness, while William Henry's commitment to justice instilled in her the drive to confront wrongs and advocate for change. Their values lived on in her, giving her the foundation she needed to navigate the challenges that lay ahead. While her brothers sought safety in passing, Ethel recognized that her Blackness was not a barrier but a source of strength. She understood that her identity was more than a label; it was an inheritance of resilience, courage, and a call to action.

The loss of William Henry in November 1948, followed by Inga's passing just two months later, marked a profound shift in the Ray family. Ethel, already a woman of conviction, now felt the full weight of her family's legacy resting on her shoulders. Her father's death brought to light tensions that had long simmered within the family, particularly around the choices her brothers had made. In the months following his death, Ethel wrote a letter to her father, pouring out her frustrations and sense of betrayal regarding her brothers' decisions to live as white men. She recalled an exchange with Will, who had remarked, "You chose the right road—marrying colored was the right decision for you." Ethel responded with a mix of bitterness and pride. "Who is he to tell me what is right or wrong in my life?" she wrote, questioning the authority of a brother who had turned his back on his heritage.

In their mother's absence, Will confessed that he and Oscar finally felt a sense of "freedom," revealing the internalized shame and struggle that had defined their lives. This admission stirred a mix of clarity and sadness in Ethel, underscoring the different ways each sibling had processed the complexities of their identities. While her brothers had spent their lives evading the pain of racial discrimination,

Ethel had embraced her heritage, finding purpose in her father's vision of justice.

William Henry's life had been guided by a commitment to justice that transcended personal safety. He saw it as his duty to fight not only for his own family but for all Black people who faced oppression. His journey from the South to Duluth in 1899, a region that would soon experience the horror of racial violence, only deepened his resolve. For him, survival was not enough—it required action and sacrifice. His life embodied the belief that dignity and progress came from standing up to injustice, regardless of the risks. This conviction became his legacy, one that Ethel would carry forward.

Ethel sometimes found her father's stance rigid, even frustrating, yet she respected his vision and the values he had instilled in her. His love for her, combined with his belief in justice, gave her the strength to pursue a life of advocacy and civil rights work. With his passing, Ethel took up his torch, determined to honor his legacy. Her work in activism and her steadfast commitment to her Black identity became a testament to the principles he had lived by. William Henry had taught her that true courage came from embracing one's identity and standing firm in the face of oppression—a lesson that became the foundation of her life's work.

This legacy of resilience and advocacy extended beyond Ethel to future generations. Her son, Glenn Ray Nance, took up the mantle, ensuring that the fight for justice would not end with her. Ethel's life and work provided a bridge between the past and the future, grounding her family's story in the pursuit of dignity and equality. Each generation took on the responsibility to carry forward these values, honoring the sacrifices and achievements of those who came before.

EPILOGUE: A LIFE DEDICATED TO JUSTICE

Ethel's commitment to justice carried her far beyond the confines of her hometown, transforming her into a figure of national significance. In January 1923, Ethel left Duluth for St. Paul, stepping onto a path that would shape her future and expand her reach across the country. After five months clerking at the Minnesota State Capitol, she joined civic and social organizations that focused on serving Black communities. Her journey took her from Kansas City to Chicago, New York, Seattle, and ultimately to San Francisco, where she would settle in 1944 and remain until her death in 1992 at the age of ninety-three.

Her contributions spanned numerous roles, each one underscoring her dedication to civil rights and community service. She became Minneapolis's first Black policewoman, a groundbreaking position that challenged the conventions of her time. She also served as an administrative assistant with the NAACP, working alongside key figures in the fight for racial equality. Perhaps one of her most remarkable roles was as secretary to W. E. B. Du Bois at the founding of the United Nations, a historic event that symbolized a new era of global advocacy for human rights. In each role, Ethel exemplified the strength and commitment her father had instilled in her, using her voice and position to advocate for justice and equality.

Appendix

Timeline

The Black Population in Minnesota

List of Images

References and Resources

Timeline

1861

US Civil War begins (April 12)

1865

US Civil War ends (April 9)

Ku Klux Klan founded in Pulaski, Tennessee (December 24)

Reconstruction occurs (1865–1877)

1868

William Henry Ray born in Oberlin, North Carolina, now known as Raleigh, North Carolina

1870

Inga Nordquist born in Eksharad, Varmland County, Sweden

1872

Henry Ray (William Henry's father) dies. William Henry was four years old.

1877

Reconstruction ends and federal troops withdraw from the South.

1878

William Henry leaves North Carolina. He is ten years old.

1879

William Henry arrives in Davenport, Iowa. He is eleven years old.

1888

Inga immigrates to United States and begins working at Ardmore Hotel in Minneapolis. She is seventeen years old.

William Henry begins working at Ardmore Hotel (August 23). He is twenty years old.

1889

Courtship between William Henry and Inga begins (March 7)

Inga leaves Ardmore Hotel and begins work as a domestic (May 3)

William Henry leaves Ardmore Hotel and begins work on the railroad (June)

Inga is pregnant (October)

1890

William Henry and Inga move to Duluth and rent a house (February 6)

William Henry begins work at Spalding Hotel (February 7)

William Henry and Inga marry (May 14)

William "Will" Nordquist Ray, their first child, born in Duluth (June 23)

Ray family moves to Two Harbors; William Henry and Inga work at a boardinghouse.

1893

Ora Inga Ray, their second child, born in Two Harbors (January)

1895

Oscar Edwin Ray, their third child, born in Two Harbors (January 25)

1898

Ray family moves back to Duluth and buys a home at 209 East 5th Street

1899

Ethel May Ray, their fourth and last child, born in Duluth (April 13)

1900

Ora dies (October 1) of pneumonia. She was seven years old.

1905

Ethel attends kindergarten and first grade at Franklin Elementary (1905–1907)

1907

Franklin Elementary burns down; Ethel attends second through eighth grades at Nettleton Elementary (1907–1914).

1910

John Beargrease dies.

1914

World War I begins in Europe (June 28)

Ethel attends Duluth Central High (1914–1917)

Ethel takes civil service examinations for stenographer during high school.

1917

United States enters World War I (April 6)

Ethel graduates from Duluth Central High School (June 13)

1918

Ethel works as stenographer and investigator for Minnesota Forest Fire Relief Commission in Moose Lake, while also working as secretary for Charles Mahnke at the Moose Lake Star-Gazette (October 1918–March 1919)

World War I ends (November 11)

Ethel returns to Moose Lake to fill in for a sick colleague - Minnesota Forest Fire Relief Commission (December)

1919

Ethel works at Minnesota Forest Fire Relief Commission in Moose Lake (March 1919–August 1922)

Ethel travels with her father around the country on a four-month trip (December 1919–March 1920)

1920

A mob in Duluth lynches three Black men—Elias Clayton, Elmer Jackson, and Isaac McGhie (June 15). Ethel is twenty-one years old.

1921

NAACP founding member W. E. B. Du Bois speaks to the citizens of Duluth (March 21)

1922

Ethel returns to Duluth after three years working in Moose Lake

1923

Ethel Ray leaves Duluth for St. Paul and becomes Minnesota State Legislature's first African American stenographer (January–May)

1923

Ethel works for Kansas City Urban League

Ethel attends summer school in Chicago with National Playground Association

1924

During Harlem Renaissance, Ethel works for Charles Johnson at National Urban League in New York City (May 1924–November 1925)

1926

Phyllis Wheatley House in Minneapolis hires Ethel as assistant head resident (March)

1928

Ethel becomes Minneapolis Police Department's first African American policewoman—and first African American policewoman in state. (April 1928–January 1931)

1929

Ethel marries LeRoy Alexis Herbert Williams in Anoka, Minnesota (August 3)

1933

Thatcher Popel Willliams, Ethel's first child, was born in Washington, D.C. (January 11). During Ethel's pregnancy, she suffered a cataclysmic attack of acute arthritis that left her with a limp. This led her to quit the police department. At this time her husband also lost his job and accepted his family's offer to come to Maryland to live with them.

1934

Glenn Ray Williams, Ethel's second child, born in Duluth, Minnesota

Ethel serves as Assistant to Director of Unemployment Survey under ERA (Equal Rights Amendments)

1935

Ethel returns to Twin Cities to work for Minnesota Negro Council (January–April)

1937

Ethel works for Minnesota Department of Education (April 1937–September 1940)

1940

Ethel works for Hampton Institute in Virginia (1940–1943)

1943

Ethel and LeRoy divorce (February 18)

1944

Ethel marries Clarence Aristotle Nance in Seattle (February 2)

Thatcher and Glenn, Ethel's sons, change their last name to Nance.

1945

Nance family moves to San Francisco, California

Founding conference of the United Nations held in San Fransisco; Ethel works as secretary for W. E. B. Du Bois, who represents the NAACP as a consultant to American delegation (April 25–June 26).

Ethel serves as Special Administrative Assistant at NAACP Regional Office in San Francisco (1945–1955)

1948

William Henry Ray dies in San Francisco while visiting his daughter Ethel Ray Nance on November 27

1949

Inga Nordquist Ray dies in Duluth.

1951

Ethel becomes a member of California Bay Area NAACP–GI Assistance Committee

1963

Oscar dies

1970

Will Norquist dies

1971

Ethel is a member of Advisory Committee of a joint project with Bancroft Library at University of California, Berkeley, and NAACP Regional Office on a Repository of Historical Documents

1978

At seventy-nine years old, Ethel becomes oldest individual to receive a bachelor's degree from University of San Francisco

1992

Ethel passes away at the age of ninety-three (July 11)

Black Population In Minnesota

The Black population in Minnesota has historically been small. According to the census in 1890, the state's total population was 1,310,283, and the Black population was 3,683—only 0.3 percent. The state's Black population remained below 1 percent for many years. Still, it began growing significantly between 1950 and 1970, during the last phase of the Great Migration of African Americans from Southern states to the North, Midwest, and West. Although Minnesota's Black population did not increase as much as the populations of other Northern states such as Illinois and Michigan, it rose by 149 percent during these twenty years. In 1980, the state's total population was 4,075,970, and its Black population was 53,344 (1.3 percent). By 2020, the census reported Minnesota's total population as 5,706,494 compared to the Black population of 398,494—about 7 percent of the total population. The second migration of Black people to Minnesota from 1990 to 2020 is due to the influx of diverse Black populations immigrating from Africa, particularly Somalia, Ethiopia, and the Caribbean. "Black" is defined as self-chosen for census purposes. The data of the Black population reported here does not simply include African Americans who have been in the United States for twenty-five generations but, rather, includes multi-ethnicities and nationalities who see Black as their primary identity for counting purposes.

In the decade after the Duluth lynchings, between 1920 and 1930, the white population of Duluth increased by at least 2,000 people, and the city's Black population dropped from 495 to 416, a decrease of 16 percent. In fact, Black people didn't start repopulating Duluth until the 1950s, after at least a generation of erasure of the 1920 violence had occurred. The decrease in Duluth's Black population from 1920 to 1950 was 33 percent, or a third, of its Black community. However, from 1950 to 1960, there was a 40 percent increase in Black people living in Duluth.

Black Populations in Minnesota 1890 - 2020

Year	Duluth	St. Paul	Minneapolis	Minnesota
1890	155	1,624	1,317	3,683
1900	264	2,263	1,616	4,959
1910	410	3,144	2,712	7,084
1920	495	3,376	3,806	8,809
1930	416	4,001	4,179	9,445
1940	309	4,139	4,431	9,928
1950	334	5,655	6,782	14,022
1960	555	8,240	11,589	22,263
1970	857	10,848	19,114	34,868
1980	742	13,242	28,564	53,344
1990	697	19,435	46,467	94,944
2000	1,390	33,637	67,966	171,731
2010	1,988	43,615	70,011	282,791
2020	1,988	51,402	81,262	398,494

Population in Minnesota 1890 - 2020

Year	Duluth	St. Paul	Minneapolis	Minnesota
1890	33,115	135,156	164,738	1,310,283
1900	52,969	163,065	202,718	1,751,394
1910	78,466	214,744	301,408	2,075,708
1920	98,917	234,698	380,582	2,387,125
1930	101,453	271,606	464,370	2,563,953
1940	101,065	287,736	521,718	2,792,300
1950	104,511	311,349	482,872	2,982,483
1960	107,312	313,411	434,400	3,413,864
1970	105,078	309,980	370,951	3,804,971
1980	92,811	270,230	368,383	4,075,970
1990	85,493	272,235	382,618	4,375,099
2000	86,918	287,151	382,578	4,919,479
2010	86,265	285,068	429,954	5,303,925
2020	86,697	311,527	425,336	5,706,494

US Census Bureau, census.gov
Census Decennial Publications for Minnesota, General Population Characteristics 1890–2020

LIST OF IMAGES

Photo of young William Henry Ray, circa 1880s   Page 20

Ethel Ray Nance Family Archive

Karen Felecia Nance, San Francisco, California

Photo of William Henry and Inga Ray, 1889   Page 22

Ethel Ray Nance Family Archive

Karen Felecia Nance, San Francisco, California

Will, Inga and Oscar after the Funeral of Ora, 1900   Page 27

(Photo by William Henry)

Ethel Ray Nance Family Archive

Karen Felecia Nance, San Francisco, California

Advertisement for John Robinson's Circus   Page 53

Duluth Herald, June 10, 1920, page 11.

From Minnesota Historical Society, MNOPEDIA

mnhs.org/sites/default/files/records/documents/00001835.pdf

African Dodger Game Flier	**Page 66**
Kelly, Erin. (2023). "The History of Racist Carnival Games Like 'African Dodger'	
allthatsinteresting.com/african-dodger	
Lynching in Duluth, Minnesota postcard, 1920	**Page 73-74**
Newspaper clippings regarding the Duluth lynchings	**Pages 75-76**
"Minnesota's Disgrace" by Editor	
The Appeal (St. Paul and Minneapolis, Minnesota), June 19, 1920, page 2.	
Black owned	
Photo of Ethel Ray, circa 1920	**Page 94**
Ethel Ray Nance Family Archive	
Karen Felecia Nance, San Francisco, California	
"Colored girl is appointed clerk in legislature"	**Page 100**
The Appeal (St. Paul and Minneapolis, Minnesota), December 13, 1922	

References And Resources

Ethel Ray Nance Archive
San Francisco, California
Housed and owned by Karen Felecia Nance

"Nance, Ethel Ray (1899–1992)"
MNOPEDIA
mnopedia.org/person/nance-ethel-ray-1899-1992

St. Mark's African Methodist Episcopal Church
Duluth, Minnesota
stmark-ame.org/history

Fedo, Michael, *The Lynchings in Duluth*, Second edition
Minnesota Historical Society Press, St. Paul, Minnesota

The Appeal, St. Paul and Minneapolis, Minnesota 1920–1923
African American weekly newspaper, John Quincy Adams, editor

Ouse, David. "Ethel Ray Nance." *Zenith City Online*, February 13, 2014

Zenith City Press, Duluth, Minnesota
zenithcity.com/archive/people-biography/ethel-ray-nance

Minnesota Black History Project: Interview with Ethel Ray Nance
Oral History Collection, Minnesota Historical Society, St. Paul, Minnesota
Description: Mrs. Nance discusses her family background, the Duluth black community in the early 1900s, the 1920 lynchings in Duluth, the Moose Lake Fire Relief Commission (1918) and her work experiences. OH 43.16

Ethel Ray Nance Papers, 1895–1979
Manuscript Collection, Minnesota Historical Society, St. Paul, Minnesota
Description: Includes newspaper clippings, correspondence, and biographical information on Ethel Ray Nance. P1852

Duluth Lynchings: Resources relating to the tragic events of June 15, 1920

Minnesota Historical Society, St. Paul, Minnesota

mnhs.org/duluthlynchings

www.ingramcontent.com/pod-product-compliance
Lightning Source LLC
LaVergne TN
LVHW072337080526
838199LV00109B/447